# A TUSCAN TABLE

Buon Appetito

A Gift from
Diane Johnson

# *A*

# *TUSCAN*

# *TABLE*

## The Secrets of Three Generations of Tuscan Family Cooking

By Diane (DeAnna) Marguerite Johnson

*To my Mother Marguerite who I watched make many of these dishes when I was a child, and taught me how to cook and to enjoy the pleasures of dining with family and friends, and my sweetheart Bobby who helped me record many recipes and tasted every one usually many times, and to my son Jason who was always a delight to have in the kitchen as he grew up and refined many of the dishes in this book and, to my grandsons Evan and Leighton who already enjoy the preparation of food and the fine art of Italian dining, and to my daughter-in-law Molly who is a true and talented Italian cook.*

*Also to my late Father who complimented my Mother on her cooking after every diner, and then gave her a kiss.*

# VI

# A Tuscan Table

# *CONTENTS*

*Appetizers - Antipasti*

*Bread and Pizza - Pane and Pizza*

*Soups-Zuppa*

*First Courses - Primi Piatti*

*Side Dishes – Contorni*

*Miscellaneous – Aggegi vari*

*Entrees - Secondi Piatti*

*Salads - Insalata*

*Cheese Course - Formaggi*

*Sweets - Dolci*

*Index*

My family loves to gather at the table to enjoy good food and good conversation. The table is such a great place for families to come together and share their experiences of the day, and especially for children to participate in the conversation. At our table, conversation always seems to include food, with topics such as where to find the best ingredients, and what is each child's favorite dish that is being served at the table. Ideas are exchanged on how to prepare any given dish.

I hope you enjoy this book and that the dishes become favorites at your own homes. Many of the dishes are very quick and easily prepared with quality healthful ingredients. I wish you happy and healthy dining.

# Appetizers

*Antipasti*

Antipasti of Crudités and Olive Oil

*Pinzimonio*

This makes for a beautiful start to a celebratory meal. As this is so easy it also is a perfect way to start any meal. A variety of olives makes a nice accompaniment to these antipasti.

7 celery stalks and the tender celery leaves from the center of the celery

7 carrots

1 bulb of fennel (optional)

10 radishes

extra virgin olive oil

salt and freshly ground pepper

Rinse all of the vegetables. Remove the root end of the celery and cut off the tips by about ¼ of an inch, if the tips are dried out. Remove all tough strings from the stalks by placing your knife under the strings and pulling them lengthwise down the celery stalk. Alternatively, remove the strings with a vegetable peeler by shaving a thin layer off. Cut the celery into sticks of 1/3 inch by 3 inches approximately. The tender shoots in the center can be just cut into pieces of about 3 inches. Cut the ends off of the carrots and peel them. Cut the carrots into about the same size sticks as the celery. Cut off the top of the fennel and reserve the fennel fronds for something else. Cut off the bottom of the fennel bulb and remove the hard core. You will see that it is triangular in shape, you can easily remove it with your knife by cutting on either side of it and it will come out in one piece as a wedge. Remove any discolored outer layers. Cut the outer layers of the fennel bulb into strips and the tender inner layers into small wedges. Cut off the tops and bottoms of the radishes, if they are large you may want to cut them in half. Place all of the vegetables in serving dishes, and the olive oil in individual serving plates. Have salt and pepper available. The vegetables can be dipped into the olive oil and seasoned to the individuals taste.

Tuscan Oranges

*Arancia Tuscano*

These make a beautiful start to any celebratory meal. They are served in my family at every holiday including birthdays.

large shallow serving bowl or dish

3 to 5 oranges

brandy (use one that is of excellent quality)

1 to 2 tsp. white sugar

Peel the oranges, removing all of the white pith. Slice the oranges into slices of about ¼ inch thick, or you may slice all of the oranges except one and supreme that one. Instructions on how to supreme an orange are on page 108. Cover the bottom of a shallow serving dish with one layer of the slices without crowding them. If you are using a supremed orange arrange the supremed sections attractively around the edge of the serving bowl, and pour the juice left from supreming the orange over the orange slices and sections. Lightly sprinkle with the sugar. Pour the brandy over all of the oranges until the brandy is about ¼ inch deep. The brandy should not completely cover the oranges. Let the oranges macerate in the sugar and brandy at room temperature for approximately 1 hour then turn over all the orange pieces and let sit for another hour.

Serve as a part of an antipasti course, and if there are any left, put them out after dinner, people will come back to these.

Endive with Avocado and Sour Cream

*Indiva belga con avacodo*

1 avocado

1 head Belgian endive

½ cup sour cream

¼ cup very finely chopped chives

juice of 2 limes or 2 lemons

sea salt and freshly ground pepper to taste

Rinse the endive and place 10 spears on a serving plate. Juice the limes or lemons. Have all the ingredients out and ready to use as soon as the avocado is sliced. Avocados oxidize very quickly and start turning brown, so you want to sprinkle the lime or lemon juice on the avocado slices as quickly as possible. Cut the avocados in half lengthwise. Remove the pit. Cut the avocados into thin lengthwise slices. Place the slices on a cutting surface, and go around the edge just inside the skin and remove it. Sprinkle a few drops of lime or lemon juice on the avocado slices as you go. Place 1 slice of avocado in each spear of endive. Sprinkle a few more drops of lime or lemon juice on the avocado slices. Place a teaspoon of sour cream on each avocado slice and sprinkle a few chopped chives on top of each. Next sprinkle a little sea salt and pepper over the top of them.

## Prosciutto Wrapped Fruit Slices

*Prosciutto con frutta*

Many fruits complement the salty taste of prosciutto. Cantaloupe, honeydew melon, apples and pears are all very good. This is easy to put together and lends itself well as an antipasti for a group or as a healthy afternoon snack for adults and children.

10 thin slices of the fruit of your choice (cantaloupe, honeydew melon, apple, or pear)

10 slices of prosciutto

10 thin slices of cheese, (cut into 1 inch by 2 inch strips) such as Provolone, or Asiago.

Peel and slice whichever fruit you are using. Place a prosciutto slice on a flat surface and lay a slice of fruit and a strip of cheese crosswise on one of the short ends of the prosciutto. Roll up the fruit and cheese in a prosciutto slice and lay seam side down on a serving plate. Repeat.

If you are using this as an antipasti for a group, a variety of fruits can be used, as well as more than 1 type of cheese.

Beans Wrapped in Prosciutto

*Fagiolini verdi e prosiutto*

½ Lb. slender and tender green beans (such as haricots verts)

10 slices Prosciutto Di Parma or other prosciutto (the slices should be very thin)

extra virgin olive oil

kosher salt and freshly ground black pepper

Rinse the beans and snap off the ends and pull the strings off. Place the beans in salted boiling water and blanch for 2 minutes. Remove from the water with a slotted spoon and let them cool down enough to handle comfortably. Place a little olive oil in a dish and place the beans in the oil. Roll them around until they are coated on all sides with the oil. Lightly coat a glass or ceramic baking dish with olive oil and set aside. Take a slice of prosciutto and place 4 or 5 beans on one of the small ends of the prosciutto and roll the prosciutto around the beans. Place the rolls with the seam side down in the baking dish. Sprinkle with salt and pepper. Place in a preheated 350 degree oven for 5 minutes. Remove from the oven and serve.

## Toasted Garlic Bread

*Fettunta*

This is the Tuscan version of bruschetta. This is a version that is much loved in my family.

4 slices approximately 1 inch thick of Italian Bread (page 20,) or good quality bakery Italian or French bread

4 cloves of garlic, peeled and cut in half

extra virgin olive oil

salt and freshly ground black pepper to taste

Pre-heat the oven to 350 degrees Fahrenheit. Place the slices of bread on a sheet pan or a cookie sheet and place in the oven. When the bread starts to become toasted, turn the slices over and wait for the second side to start to firm up, then remove the bread from the oven and rub the garlic on the bread. Drizzle a little olive oil over the slices, and return to the oven. When the bread becomes slightly golden and fragrant with the olive oil, remove from the oven. Serve while still warm, with salt and freshly ground pepper available for each person to season his or her own slice of fettunta.

Toasted Garlic Bread with Fresh Tomatoes and Ricotta Salata

*Fettunta al pomodoro*

This fettunta  a Tuscan variation of bruschetta is best with tomatoes just picked from the garden, but as long as you can find good quality fresh tomatoes it will be wonderful. This makes for a refreshing and light summer lunch. Tomatoes and basil picked from the garden and brought into the kitchen for this bruschetta is like tasting summer itself.

6 slices each 1 inch thick of Italian Bread (page 20) or good quality bakery Italian or French bread

1 peeled clove of garlic

extra virgin olive oil

2 fresh tomatoes

fresh Italian basil if available otherwise any other fresh basil is fine

2 to 3 oz. of ricotta salata cut into pieces of about ½ inch by ¼ inch

sea salt or kosher salt and freshly ground black pepper to taste

Place the bread on a cookie sheet or a rimmed sheet pan, and toast in a pre-heated 350-degree oven for about 3 minutes, then turn the slices over and toast on the other side for another 3 minutes or so. When the breads surface starts to firm up, remove from the oven and rub the peeled clove of garlic over the top side of each slice of bread. Drizzle a little olive oil over all of the slices. Return to the oven for a minute just to heat and bring out the aroma and flavor of the garlic and the olive oil. When the bread is fragrant and slightly golden remove it from the oven. Place a slice or two of tomato on each slice of bread (enough to cover the bread). Place 1 or two leaves of basil that has been torn into pieces on top of the tomato. Place a few pieces of ricotta salata on top of the fettunta and sprinkle on the salt and pepper to taste.

## Cheese Crisps

*Fricos*

These are wonderful by themselves served with wine, or served with Italian Bread (page 20) or French bread or the Toasted Garlic Bread Fettunta ( page 7) and also with soup or broth. They are best served warm.

1 cup finely grated Parmigiano-Reggiano or Grana Padano cheese

Place several, tablespoon sized mounds of grated cheese in a skillet, as many as comfortably fit with about 2 inches of space around each cheese mound. Gently flatten them with a spatula; there should still be an inch of space around each frico. Cook for a minute or two. Run a spatula under the edges to loosen it from the skillet. Remove from the heat and let them harden a little. Carefully turn them over and return to the heat for a minute or so until the cheese is firm. Remove from the heat, and gently transfer to an oven proof serving platter. Place in a warm oven until you are ready to serve them.

Potato Chips

*Chips di patate*

5 russet potatoes

olive oil enough to coat potatoes on both sides

sea salt

malt vinegar or white vinegar

Slice potatoes very thinly using a mandolin or a slicing disc on a food processor. If you do not have either of these just slice as thinly as you can with a sharp knife. Lightly coat a baking sheet with the olive oil and place the potato slices in a single layer on the baking sheet. Turn each slice over to coat each side with the olive oil. Sprinkle lightly with sea salt. Do not crowd the slices so that they do not stick together when they bake. Place in a preheated 350 degree Fahrenheit oven and bake for 5 minutes, look at the slices at this time and if they are golden brown on the side touching the baking sheet, turn over each slice and continue to bake another 5 minutes or so until both sides are a beautiful golden brown.

When done sprinkle with malt vinegar or white vinegar, and sea salt and serve.

## Layered Potato Chips with Herbs

*Chips di patate con prezzemola e salvia*

3 large russet potatoes (peeled)

20 Italian parsley leaves (rinsed with stems removed)

10 fresh sage leaves (rinsed with stems removed)

1 leek white part only cut in half lengthwise and thoroughly rinsed to remove any sand or dirt

extra virgin olive oil

Fleur de Sel or other salt and freshly ground pepper

Preheat the oven to 350 degrees Fahrenheit. Generously coat a baking sheet with olive oil.

You will need very thin slices of potatoes. You can use a mandolin or a food processor to achieve this. If using a mandolin slice the potatoes lengthwise. If you do not have a mandolin or food processor, just use a knife and slice as thinly as you can. Coat each slice of potato with olive oil. Place half of the potato slices on the prepared baking sheet. Place 1 or 2 parsley leaves or a sage leaf or a piece of leek on top of each slice of potato on the baking sheet. Cover each slice with a remaining potato slice that is the same size as the one that you are covering, and gently press down. Lightly sprinkle with salt. Cover with another baking sheet. If you are using a rimmed baking sheet you can fill it with dried beans to weigh it down. Place in a preheated oven. Bake for 6 minutes and check to see if they are golden brown. If they are not golden brown yet, place the top baking sheet back on the potatoes and bake for another 4 to 6 minutes. Remove the top baking sheet and continue baking until they are beautifully golden brown, and crisp (usually another 2 minutes). Remove from the oven and if you wish you can sprinkle a little salt on the bottom side of the potato crisps. They are ready to serve. You can prepare these ahead of time and warm them just before you want to serve them.

These go well with the Aioli on (page 116).

*Swiss or Gruyère Cheese Puffs*

*Gougère alla groviera*

These are irresistible. These are so good! I can't wait to make them again.

For the Puff Pastry (Pate au Choux) – Pasta Soffiata

9 Tbsp. butter

1 ½ cups water

pinch of salt

pinch of white pepper

1 ½ cups unbleached all-purpose flour

5 large eggs

¾ cup freshly grated Swiss or Gruyère cheese

butter for lightly coating 2 baking sheets

For the Egg Glaze

1 egg

1 tsp. cold water

For the Cheese topping

¾ cup freshly grated Swiss or Gruyère cheese

Lightly butter 2 baking sheets and set aside. Measure out the flour and stir in the pepper. Set aside. Place the butter, water, and salt in a saucepan and bring to a boil over high heat. When the butter is melted and the water is bubbling, immediately remove the saucepan from the heat. Stir in the flour pepper mixture all at once. Beat the mixture vigorously with a wooden spoon to blend thoroughly. Place over moderate heat and continue to beat vigorously until the mixture leaves the side of the pan and forms a ball, and starts to form a film on the bottom of the pan. Remove from the heat, and make a indention in the dough, and place an egg into it. Stir vigorously to incorporate, then, add the remaining eggs 1 at a time stirring vigorously after each egg. Stir in the cheese. With 2 tablespoons drop mounds of the pasta soffiata dough that are 1 to 1 ½ inches in diameter and 1 inch high onto your 2 lightly buttered baking sheets. The mounds should be at least 1 ½ inches apart.

Beat the egg and 1 tsp. cold water for the egg glaze, and brush over the tops of the dough mounds. Do not let the glaze dribble down the sides of the mounds onto the baking sheets as this will prevent them from rising. Sprinkle with the ¾ cup freshly grated Swiss or Gruyère cheese. Place in a preheated 400 degree Fahrenheit oven. Bake for about 20 minutes. They may take a minute or two longer. They should turn a golden brown and be crisp to the touch. Turn the heat down to 350 degrees and bake 10 minutes more. Let them cool down until they are just warm, and serve.

Swiss or Gruyère Cheese Puffs with Asparagus

*Gougère alla groviera con asparagi*

These are wonderful with just the chopped asparagus incorporated into the puff dough. Use any of the additional ingredients for variety.

For the Puff Pastry (Pate A Choux) – Pasta Soffiata (page 13)

½ lb. asparagus cleaned (use only the tender upper parts of the asparagus)

4 to 5 slices of thinly sliced prosciutto, chopped into a very fine dice (optional) or ½ cup sautéed pancetta chopped into a small dice (optional)

2 Tbsp. chopped chives (optional)

For the Egg Glaze

1 egg

1 tsp. cold water

Cut the asparagus into ¼ inch pieces. Blanch them in a pot of boiling water for about 1 minute or until just tender. Drain and set aside.

Prepare the puff pastry, using the recipe on page 13. If you are using prosciutto, chop it into a very fine dice. For the pancetta, heat 4 Tbsp. butter in a sauté pan and add the pancetta when the butter is hot enough to sizzle when a piece of pancetta is dropped into it. Sauté for 5 minutes until the pancetta is cooked through. Remove from the sauté pan and drain on paper towels. Add the prosciutto or pancetta right after you add the cheese. Add the chopped asparagus spears. Add the chives, if you are using them at this point. With 2 tablespoons drop mounds of dough that are 1 to 1 ½ inches in diameter and 1 inch high onto 2 lightly buttered baking sheets. The mounds should be at least 1 ½ inches apart. Beat the egg and 1 tsp. cold water for the egg glaze, and brush over the tops of the dough mounds. Do not let the glaze dribble down the sides of the mounds onto the baking sheets as this will prevent them from rising. Place on a baking sheet and place in a preheated 425 degree Fahrenheit oven for about 20 minutes. These can be served as is or filled with any of the cheese fillings on page 17.

Variations

Prosciutto or pancetta can be added to either of the following variations.

Puffs with Leeks

Leeks can be substituted for the asparagus. Use 2 large leeks (white part only). Cut off root ends and the dark green tops. Slice in half lengthwise and rinse thoroughly under running water to remove any dirt or sand from between the layers. Chop into a small dice, and add the chopped leeks after the cheese is added. Place on 2 lightly buttered baking sheets. Beat the egg and 1 tsp. cold water for the egg glaze, and brush over the tops of the dough mounds. Do not let the glaze dribble down the sides of the mounds onto the baking sheets as this will prevent them from rising. Place in a 425 degree pre-heated oven for about 20 minutes.

Chive Puffs

Chives can be substituted for the asparagus. Use ½ cup finely chopped chives, and add after you add the cheese. Place on 2 lightly buttered baking sheets. Beat the egg and 1 tsp. cold water for the egg glaze, and brush over the tops of the dough mounds. Do not let the glaze dribble down the sides of the mounds onto the baking sheets as this will prevent them from rising. Place in a pre-heated 425 degree oven and bake for about 20 minutes.

## Cheese Filling

A cheese filling can be added to any of these puffs.

Make a Bechamella (page 119) and add 1 cup of Gruyère or Swiss cheese, or if you prefer a mascarpone or cream cheese sauce you can add 1 cup mascarpone or cream cheese in place of the Gruyère or Swiss cheese. A little cayenne pepper added to taste is a nice addition if you are using mascarpone or cream cheese in the sauce. Additionally you can add blanched asparagus pieces, as described In Swiss or Gruyère Puffs with Asparagus (Page 15) or chopped chives. Another addition that is exceptionally good is ½ cup Sautéed Leeks (page 110).

To add a filling to the puffs cut a horizontal slit in the side of each puff. If the puffs have to much soft dough in them, just take out the excess dough with a small spoon or with your fingers. With a small spoon fill each puff with about a teaspoonful of filling.

Olives Baked in Pastry

*Olive con pasta*

25 olives pitted (pimento stuffed queen olives, black olives, kalamata olives or any variety that you like)

½ recipe of Pastry for A Two Crust Pie page 199

butter for coating a baking sheet

Prepare the pie dough according to directions on page 199. Butter a baking sheet and set it aside. After the dough has chilled and you have rolled it out, cut the dough into strips 3/4 inch wide and 1 ½ inches long. The strip should be just long enough to go around an olive. Place an olive crosswise on the end of a strip of pastry dough and roll the dough around the olive. The pitted ends of the olives should be visible. Place on your buttered baking sheet about ½ inch apart.

Place in a pre-heat 375 degree oven for 5 to 10 minutes until the pastry is cooked through and a light golden brown.

Remove from the oven and serve while still warm.

# Bread and Pizza

## *Pane and Pizza*

Italian Bread

*Pane*

My grandmother made Italian bread every week. Many wonderful memories can be made with the preparation of homemade bread. Children love to take part in bread making, especially punching down the dough. Making homemade bread is comforting and there is nothing like the aroma of baking bread. I am looking forward to baking this again with my young grandchildren.

2 tsp. dry yeast

½ cup warm water (110 to 115 degrees Fahrenheit)

3 ½ cups warm water (110 to 115 degrees Fahrenheit)

1 tablespoon salt

6 cups flour

4 to 4 ½ cups unbleached all-purpose flour or a little more (another ½ cup or so)

In a small bowl place the ½ cup warm water and mix in the 2 tsp. yeast, stir and let sit for 5 to 10 minutes. Mix the 3 ½ cups of warm water with the salt in a large bowl and stir. Add the 6 cups of flour and mix together. Stir the water yeast mixture and add it to the flour water mixture. Stir with a wooden spoon until it is mixed well. Add 2 cups more of the flour and mix. Add enough of the remaining flour to make a soft dough. Place the dough on a flat surface that has been lightly dusted with flour, cover with an inverted bowl and let sit for 10 minutes.

Knead: Folding the dough in half, by taking the end of the dough that is away from you and folding it towards you. Use the heel of your hand to push the dough away from yourself. Give the dough a quarter turn and repeat. Keep kneading 5 to 10 minutes, incorporating as little as possible flour as you are kneading, just enough to keep the dough from being sticky.

Place the dough in a lightly oiled bowl, that is large enough to hold the dough after it has doubled in size. Turn the dough over bringing the oiled side to the top. Cover with waxed paper and place a cotton dish towel on top of the paper. Let the dough rise in a warm place around 80 degrees Fahrenheit, until the dough is doubled in bulk (about 1 ½ hours to 2 hours.

Punch the dough down with your hand. Knead as before on a lightly floured surface for 2 to 4 minutes. Divide into four equal pieces and form each into a ball. Cover each ball with an inverted bowl or place a piece of waxed paper over each ball and then place a cotton dish towel on top of the paper. Let it rest for 10 minutes.

Roll each ball of dough into a rectangle of about 8 by 14 inches, or for a more slender loaf, roll into a rectangle of 7 by 15 inches. Roll up the long side tightly, making a long slender loaf of 14 to 15 inches. Pinch the ends to seal. Place the loaves on a lightly buttered baking sheet. Cover each loaf with waxed paper and place a cotton dish towel on top of the paper. Place in a warm place around 80 degrees Fahrenheit, and let the loaves double in size.

Place in a preheated 425 degree Fahrenheit oven for 10 minutes. Turn down the temperature to 350 degrees Fahrenheit, and bake for about an hour, or until the loaves are a beautiful golden brown.

Olive Oil Pizza (Light Crispy Pizza)

*Pizza all' olio*

This makes 2 pizzas 10 ½ by 16 inches. Pre-baking the pizza dough along with rolling the dough out very thinly and spreading just a thin layer of tomato sauce gives this pizza a light and crispy texture. This dough will puff somewhat during the pre-baking, this adds to the texture and lightness.

1 ¾ cup flour

1 ½ tsp. salt

2 Tbsp. extra-virgin olive oil (1 Tbsp for each pizza)

½ cup water

flour  for dusting baking sheet

2 tablespoon extra-virgin olive oil

1/2 cup very finely freshly grated Parmigianino- Reggiano (1/4 cup for each pizza)

1 cup tomato puree

½ cup tomato paste

8 oz. low moisture mozzarella ( 4 oz. For each pizza) cut into pieces of about ½ inch by 1 inch

4 teaspoons dried oregano (2 teaspoons for each pizza)

Mix the flour and salt together in the bowl of a stand mixer. In a small bowl mix the olive oil and water together. Using the flat beater attachment slowly add the olive oil, water mixture to the flour mixture in the mixer while it is running slowly. When the dough is mixed remove it from the mixer and place on a lightly floured surface and cover the dough and let it rest for 10 minutes.

Uncover the dough and knead it, (instructions for kneading are on page 20) for 1 minute. Divide the dough in half and shape into 2 balls. Wrap each ball with plastic wrap, and place in the refrigerator and let them rest for 1 hour.

While the dough is resting you can grate the Parmigianino and make the tomato topping. Mix the tomato puree and tomato paste together thoroughly.

Lightly dust the baking sheets with flour, and set aside. Roll out the dough as thin as you can and let it rest again for 5 to 10 minutes. Place each rolled out pizza dough on a baking sheet, and bake in a preheated 350 degrees Fahrenheit oven for 5 minutes or until the dough is lightly puffed. Remove from the oven and let it sit for 5 minutes. Spread a tablespoon of olive oil over each pizza dough with a pastry brush, and lightly sprinkle the freshly grated Parmigiano on top. Place in the oven and let bake another 5 to 10 minutes.

Remove from the oven, and spread the tomato mixture very thinly and evenly over each pizza dough and distribute the mozzarella pieces evenly on top. Rub the dried oregano in your hands to crumble it and distribute it over the pizzas.

Place in a preheated 350 degree Fahrenheit oven and bake for another 10 minutes or until the cheese is melted and starting to turn a golden brown. Remove from the oven and serve while still hot.

Margherita Pizza

*Pizza alla Margherita*

This pizza has the same dough as the Olive Oil Pizza (page 21), so this Margherita Pizza has the same light and crispy texture. The dough will puff somewhat during the pre-baking, which adds to the texture and lightness. Placing the tomatoes on top of the mozzarella forms a moisture barrier between the tomatoes and the dough and keeps the crust crispy. This makes 2 pizzas.

1 ¾ cup flour

1 ½ tsp. salt

2 Tbsp. extra-virgin olive oil (1 Tbsp. for each pizza)

½ cup water

flour for dusting baking sheet

2 tablespoon extra-virgin olive oil

1/2 cup very finely freshly grated Parmigianino-Reggiano (1/4 cup for each pizza)

8 oz. low moisture mozzarella (4 oz. For each pizza) cut into thin slices a cheese slicer works well for this

4 fresh tomatoes cut into very thin slices (vine-on tomatoes or Roma tomatoes )

12 fresh basil leaves cut into a thin strips (chiffonade)*

Mix the flour and salt together in the bowl of a stand mixer. In a small bowl mix the olive oil and water together. Using the flat beater attachment, slowly add the olive oil, water mixture to the flour mixture in the mixer while it is running slowly. When the dough is mixed remove it from the mixer and place on a lightly floured surface and cover the dough and let it rest for 10 minutes.

Uncover the dough and knead it (instructions for kneading are on page 20) for 1 minute. Divide the dough in half and shape into 2 balls. Wrap each ball with plastic wrap, and place in the refrigerator and let them rest for 1 hour.

While the dough is resting you can grate the Parmigiano.

Lightly dust the baking sheets with flour and set aside. Roll out the dough as thin as you can and let it rest again for 5 to 10 minutes. Place each pizza dough on a baking sheet, and bake in a preheated 350 degrees Fahrenheit for 5 minutes or until the dough is lightly puffed. Remove from the oven and let it sit for 5 minutes. Spread a tablespoon of olive oil over each pizza dough with a pastry brush, and lightly sprinkle the freshly grated Parmigiano on top. Place in the oven and let bake another 5 to 10 minutes. Remove from the oven, and distribute the mozzarella pieces evenly on top. Place the thinly sliced tomatoes on top of the mozzarella pieces. Take the chiffonade of basil and evenly distribute over the pizza.

Place in a preheated 350 degree Fahrenheit oven and bake for another 10 minutes or until the cheese is melted and starting to turn a golden brown. Remove from the oven and serve while still hot.

* Chiffonade (thin strips)

Stack several leaves one on top of each other all facing in the same direction and tightly roll up lengthwise, and starting at the stem end cut crosswise into thin strips. Unroll and separate the strips.

Tomato Cheese Pizza

*Pizza al formaggio e pomodoro*

Dough

1 tsp. dry yeast or

2 Tbsp. warm water 80 to 100 degrees Fahrenheit

1 cup warm water

4 cups all purpose flour

¾ tsp. salt

butter for coating 2 baking sheets

Topping

6 ripe fresh tomatoes or 8 oz. tomato puree and 8 oz. tomato paste

2 ripe fresh tomatoes thinly sliced

2 tsp. oregano

8 oz. mozzarella

For the dough

In a small bowl place the 2 Tbsp. warm water and mix in the yeast, stir and let sit for 5 to 10 minutes. Mix 2 cups of the flour with the salt in a bowl. Pour the 1 cup of warm water into a large wide bowl, blend in the flour and salt mixture. Stir the yeast mixture and add it to flour, water, salt mixture and mix well. Add about 1 cup of the remaining flour and mix until very smooth. Add in as much of the remaining 1 cup flour as you need to make a soft dough. Place on a lightly floured surface and knead: Fold the dough in half, by taking the end of the dough that is away from you and folding it towards you. Using the heel of your hand, push the dough away from yourself. Give the dough a quarter turn and repeat. Keep kneading for 5 to 10 minutes, incorporating as little flour as possible as you knead, using just enough to keep the dough from being sticky.

Place the dough in a lightly oiled bowl, one that is large enough to hold the dough after it has doubled in size. Turn the dough over bringing the oiled side to the top. Cover with waxed paper and place a cotton dish towel on top of the paper. Let the dough rise in a warm place around 80 degrees Fahrenheit until the dough is doubled in bulk (about 1 ½ to 2 hours.

Punch the dough down with your hand. Fold the edges of the dough into the center forming a ball. Turn the dough over and cut in half. Form each half into a ball. Oil a second bowl and place a ball of dough in each bowl. Turn the dough over bringing the oiled side to the top. Cover as before and let rise again, until the dough is almost double in size about 45 minutes.

Roll out each portion of dough to a 14 to 15 inch diameter circle or a 10 by 14 inch rectangle. Either should be 1/8 inch thick.

Lightly oil 2 baking sheets and place the pizza dough on them. Form a raised edge by pressing the dough between your thumb and fingers.

For the topping

If you are using fresh tomatoes pass them through a food mill to puree them. For the canned pureed tomatoes and paste, mix them together thoroughly. Spread either the pureed fresh tomatoes or the canned tomato mixture over the pizza dough. Pace the tomato slices on the pizzas, then distribute the mozzarella evenly over the top of each pizza. Drizzle the olive oil over each and then sprinkle each with the dried oregano, pepperoncino and salt.

Place in a preheated 375 degree Fahrenheit oven and bake 30 to 45 minutes or until the bottom of the crust is golden brown.

# Soups

## *Zuppa*

Brown Chicken Stock

*Brodo di pollo*

Makes about 8 cups or 1 gallon

2 Lb. chicken wings

1 lb. chicken breast

2 medium carrots peeled and chopped into 2 inch pieces

2 celery ribs cut into 3 inch pieces

1 medium leek (root removed and use only the white and light parts) quartered and rinsed under cold running water

1 medium onion peeled and cut into eighths

4 whole cloves garlic peeled

4 sprigs parsley

4 whole peppercorns

2 Tbsp. tomato paste

Rinse off the chicken pieces, and cut the chicken breast into large chunks of about 2 or 3 inches. Place all the chicken pieces in a large shallow roasting pan. Place in a preheated 375 degree Fahrenheit oven. Roast for 30 to 40 minutes turning occasionally until the chicken pieces are golden brown. Check to see how much fat is in your roasting pan, if there is more than a 1/8 inch coating, remove the excess fat. If there is hardly any fat add a little olive oil to the pan before adding the vegetables, stir to coat the vegetables in the fat. Roast until the vegetables are caramelized, about 20 minutes. Add tomato paste and stir to coat. Place roasting pan on top of the stove over low heat. Add 1 cup water and scrape up the browned bits with a wooded spoon. Transfer the contents of the roasting pan to a stockpot and cover with enough water to cover everything by 4 inches (about 6 ½ quarts of water). Add the parsley sprigs and the peppercorns. Bring slowly to a boil over medium heat. Reduce the heat so that the water is just simmering. Simmer for 1 ½ to 2 hours. Skim the surface of froth and fat as it accumulates. If the cooking liquid starts to evaporate below the level of the solid ingredients, add enough water to cover. Turn the heat off and let the stock sit for 15 minutes in order for the solids to settle to the bottom. Ladle the stock through a fine mesh sieve set over a large container. Transfer to smaller containers and refrigerate right away, so that the stock cools rapidly. Refrigerate over night and the next day you can skim off the solid fat. The stock can be kept 3 days under refrigeration. If you wish to freeze all or part of the stock, you can ladle it into ice cube trays and freeze. When the stock is frozen transfer the cubes of stock from the trays to plastic freezer bags and seal. It is a good idea to label the bags with the date they are frozen. They should keep in the freezer for up to 3 months.

Leek Broth

*Minestra con i porri*

This is so simple and so elegant. It makes a beautiful first course.

Soup

4 medium sized leeks

4 cups water or enough to cover the leeks by 2 inches

salt and freshly ground pepper to taste

Butter Crisped Leeks for Garnish

1 cup very thinly sliced leeks including the light green part (1 medium leek)

1 Tbsp. butter or enough to coat a small sauté pan

For the soup

Cut the root ends and the dark green tops off of the leeks. Make a slit running lengthwise to the center of the leeks from the top to the bottom, so that you can open up the leeks and rinse them under running water to remove any dirt or sand. Slice the leeks into thin discs. Place water in a pot and bring to a boil. Add salt and the leeks, let the water return to a boil and then turn down the heat to a gentle simmer. Let simmer for 20 to 25 minutes. While the soup is simmering prepare the garnish.

For the Butter Crisped Leeks garnish

While the soup is simmering, clean the leek for the garnish as described in the previous paragraph. Cut the leek into thin discs. Melt the butter and add the leeks when it is hot enough to sizzle when a piece of leek is added to it. Sauté until the leeks are tender, and starting to turn golden brown and crispy at the edges, about 5 to 7 minutes.

After the soup has simmered for 20 to 25 minutes, remove it from the heat and let it cool down enough to eat before serving. Place in individual bowls and serve with the leek garnish.

The Cheese Crisps (page 9) go very well with this, as well as a slice of Italian Bread (page 20) or Toasted Garlic Bread (page 7).

Leek and Potato Soup

*Minestra di porri e patate*

The predominant flavor in this soup is the delicate taste of leeks. This soup is a favorite of my family.

2 cups russet potatoes peeled and cut into chunks (3 medium potatoes)

4 cups sliced leeks including the light green part (6 medium sized leeks)

6 cups water

1 Tbsp. kosher salt

¼ cup whipping cream (optional)

salt and freshly ground pepper to taste

Butter Crisped Leeks for Garnish page 32

For the soup

Cut off the root ends and the dark green tops of the leeks. Slice in half lengthwise and rinse under running water to remove any dirt or sand. Cut the leeks into strips. Place the water in a large pot and bring to a boil, add the kosher salt, potato chunks and the cut up leeks. Bring to a boil and then reduce the heat and let simmer for 30 to 35 minutes.

While the potatoes and leeks are simmering prepare the Leek Garnish on page 32.

When the potatoes are tender enough to be easily pierced with a knife, remove the pot from the heat and let cool slightly. Place the potatoes and leeks in a food processor and pulse on and off until pureed. The soup is very good at this point and can be served as it is, or you can add the optional ¼ cup of cream, which gives the soup a luxurious creamy taste. It does not take much cream to achieve this.

To serve, place in soup bowls and place a few Butter Crisped Leeks on top of each serving.

## Squash Soup

extra virgin olive oil for coating a baking sheet

2 medium sized butternut squash (about 3 to 3 ½ lbs.)

4 Tbsp. butter

1 medium sized onion root ends cut off, peeled and cut into a ½ inch dice

4 or 5 stalks celery rinsed. Tips, root ends, and strings removed ( instructions on page 2) then cut into a ½ inch dice about 1 cup

4 or 5 carrots ends removed, peeled and cut into a ½ inch dice (about 1 cup)

4 cups Brown Chicken Stock (page 30), or organic purchased chicken stock

1 to 2 tsp. sour cream per serving (optional)

Lightly coat a baking sheet with olive oil, and set aside. Cut each butter nut squash in half horizontally cutting the long neck off of each squash, then cut each piece in half lengthwise. Remove the seeds and strings from the squash. Place the squash cut side down on a baking sheet. Bake in a preheated 350 degree oven for about 45 minutes, or until the squash flesh is easily pierced with a fork. Remove from the oven and let it cool.

Heat the butter in a large soup pot. Add the onions when the butter is hot enough to sizzle when a piece of onion is dropped into it. Sauté for a minute or so and add the diced carrot, and the diced celery. Sauté until the onion is translucent and the carrots and celery are cooked through. Scoop out the squash flesh and add it to the soup pot and stir to combine. Add the chicken stock and bring to a boil, then reduce the heat and simmer for 15 minutes. Turn off the heat and let the soup cool down for fifteen minutes or so, then puree in a food processor. Pour the soup back into the soup pot and gently simmer for a few minutes. Ladle into soup bowls and if you wish place a dollop of sour cream on top of each serving, the sour cream can be swirled into the soup for a rich creamy taste.

# First Course

## *Primi Piatti*

## Fettuccini with Capers, Black Olives, Mushrooms and Parsley

*Fettuccine con olive nere, capperi, prezzemolo e funghi*

1/2 cup extra virgin olive oil or a little more

1 head of garlic peeled and finely minced

2 packages (8 oz. each) of white button mushrooms (peeled- optional- instructions on page 46) and rinsed or 16 oz. of assorted mushrooms, rinsed and coarsely chopped

1 teaspoon of peperoncinio (red pepper flakes)

20 oil-cured black olives or 1 can 5 ¾ oz. colossal black olives cut into fourths

1 bottle of capers 3.5 oz.

1/3 cup of rinsed and chopped parsley leaves

salt and freshly ground pepper to taste

1 lb. package (16 oz.) of dry fettuccini

1 Tbsp. kosher salt for the pasta water

Parmigiano-Reggiano

Place a large pot of water on to boil. When it reaches a boil add the kosher salt and the pasta, return to a boil, and cook according to the package directions until al dente (tender but firm to the bite).

Meanwhile as the water heats up, place the mushrooms in a small pan over medium heat and cook them until they are soft and aromatic. Heat the olive oil in a large sauté pan or skillet that is large enough to hold all of pasta once it is cooked, over medium heat. Place the finely minced garlic into the olive oil once it has reached the point that it sizzles when a piece of garlic is dropped into it. Add the peperoncinio, and watch the garlic very closely to see that it does not burn. When the garlic becomes a beautiful golden color, add the chopped olives and a little liquid, either liquid from the can if you are using canned olives or a little of the pasta cooking water if you are using oil-cured olives. Add the capers and stir. When everything is thoroughly hot, add the parsley and a little more pasta cooking water if is needed. Add the salt and pepper to taste. Turn the heat very low and cook for a minute or so. When the pasta is al-dente remove it from the water using a tongs and add it to the sauce. With your tongs toss the pasta together with the sauce. Serve immediately with freshly grated Parmigiano-Reggiano on the side.

## Linguini with Lemon Juice, Parsley and Black Olives

*Linguini con limone e prezzemolo*

1/3 cup extra virgin olive oil

2 cloves garlic peeled and very finely chopped

20 black olives cut into fourths

¾ cup curly parsley (washed)

juice of one lemon (about 1 ½ Tbsp.)

freshly ground black pepper to taste

1 lb.package (16 oz.) linguini

1 Tbsp. kosher salt for the pasta cooking water

Place a large pot of water on to boil. When it reaches a boil add the kosher salt and the pasta, return to a boil, and cook according to package directions until al dente (tender but firm to the bite). Meanwhile as the water heats up, heat the olive oil in a large sauté pan or skillet that is large enough to hold all the pasta once it is cooked, over medium heat. Place the finely chopped garlic into the olive oil once it has reached the point that it sizzles when a piece of garlic is dropped into it. Watch the garlic very closely to make sure that it does not burn. It should only turn golden. When the garlic is a beautiful golden color add the olives and a little liquid either a little liquid from the can if using canned black olives or a little of the pasta cooking water, if you are using oil cured olives. As the olives cook chop the parsley, and when the olives are thoroughly hot all the way thorough add the parsley. Add a little pasta cooking water if it is needed. When the pasta is al-dente remove it from the water using a tongs and add it to the sauce. With your tongs gently toss the pasta together with the sauce. Add the lemon juice and black pepper. Place in a large warm bowl and serve.

Spaghetti with Garlic Olive Oil, and Pepperoncino

*Spagetti aglio, olio e pepperoncino*

½ cup extra virgin olive oil or a little more

1 head of garlic peeled and finely minced

1 tsp. peperoncino (red pepper flakes)

1/3 cup chopped fresh parsley (optional)

salt and freshly ground pepper to taste

1 lb.package (16 oz.) dry spaghetti

1 Tbsp. kosher salt for the pasta water

Parmigiano-Reggiano

Place a large pot of water on to boil. When it reaches a boil add the kosher salt and the pasta, return to a boil and cook according to package directions until al dente (tender but firm to the bite). Meanwhile as the water heats up, heat the olive oil in a large sauté pan or skillet that is large enough to hold all of the pasta once it is cooked, over medium heat. Place the finely minced garlic into the olive oil once it is hot enough to sizzle when a piece of garlic is dropped into the olive oil. Watch the garlic very closely to make sure that it does not burn. It should only turn golden. Add the peperoncino and stir with a wooden spoon. When the garlic is a beautiful golden color you may add the optional parsley. When the pasta has reached the al dente stage add it to the olive oil sauce in your sauté pan with a pair of tongs. Toss the pasta with your tongs and add a little of the pasta cooking water if necessary. Place in a large warm bowl and serve.

Serves 6

Fresh Tomato Sauce

*Sugo di pomodoro fresco*

This should be made when you have access to good quality fresh tomatoes such as from your garden or a farmers market and sometimes vine-on tomatoes from the grocery store.

¼ cup extra virgin olive oil

7 Lb. fresh tomatoes

1 whole head of garlic peeled and finely chopped

2 large onions peeled and cut into a medium dice

½ tsp. chopped fresh rosemary (optional)

1 Tbsp. fresh basil cut into a fine chiffonade instructions on page 24

½ tsp salt or to taste and freshly ground black pepper to taste

1 tsp. sugar if needed

1 lb. package (16 oz.) dried long pasta such as spaghetti

1 Tbsp. kosher salt for the pasta cooking water

1 cup finely grated Parmigiano-Reggiano

Place a large pot of water on to boil. When it reaches a boil add the kosher salt and the pasta, return to a boil, and cook according to package directions until al dente (tender but firm to the bite). While the pasta is cooking, in a large pot heat the olive oil until it sizzles when a piece of garlic is dropped into it. Add the garlic and gently sauté, being very careful not to let it brown. After a minute or so, add the diced onion. Watch closely to make sure that the garlic turns only a very light golden color, and the onion only becomes translucent. Add the chopped tomatoes, and chopped fresh rosemary if you are using it. Cook stirring frequently for 5 minutes. Taste and if the sauce is sweet and fresh tasting, it is done. Stir in the fresh basil. Remove 2 cups of sauce and place it in a serving bowl. When the pasta is al-dente remove it from the cooking water using a tongs and add it to the sauce. With your tongs gently toss the pasta together with the sauce. Place in a large serving dish and serve immediately. Place the bowl of reserved sauce on the table, along with a bowl of finely grated Parmigiano on the table for everyone to help themselves.

Marinara Sauce

*Sugo di pomodoro*

This sauce can be used on spaghetti or linguini or in Marinara Lasagna, Eggplant Lasagne or on polenta.

Make this when you have some time to spend in the kitchen. The aroma will fill your home, and bring your family and guests into the kitchen. If you wish to have sauce left for future meals, only prepare half or less of the pasta. The sauce will keep very well for 3 days and you can prepare some pasta whenever you want to have this dish.

Serves 6 as a main course or 12 as a first course

¼ cup extra virgin olive oil

1 head of garlic peeled and finely minced

2 medium onions or 1 large onion peeled and chopped into a small dice

2 packages (8 oz.) button mushrooms (peeled* -optional), rinsed and the ends of the stems removed if they are dry looking

3 cans 1lb. 12 oz. each plum tomatoes (preferably San Marzano)

1 tsp. red pepper flakes

2 tsp. dried oregano

1 tsp. dried onion powder

1/3 cup rinsed and chopped parsley leaves

salt and freshly ground pepper to taste

1 tsp. sugar

1 lb. package (16 oz.) dried spaghetti or linguine

1 Tbsp. kosher salt for the pasta cooking water

1 cup finely grated Parmiagiano-Reggiano

Heat the olive oil in a large heavy bottomed pot. Add the garlic when the oil is hot enough to sizzle when a piece of minced garlic is dropped into it, and gently sauté for a minute, then add the chopped onion. Watch carefully to make sure that the garlic turns only a golden color and the onion only becomes translucent and does not turn brown. Cut the mushrooms into quarters and place in a small pot, and place over medium heat. The water contained in the mushrooms themselves should be sufficient to cook them. Keep an eye on them as you are sautéing the garlic and onions and turn the heat off when the mushrooms are cooked. Add the plum tomatoes to the pot with the onions and garlic and break them up with a potato masher or a wooden spoon. You can break up the tomatoes in a large bowl before adding them to the pot if you wish. A potato masher makes quick work of this. Stir over medium heat until the sauce starts to bubble, then lower the heat so that the sauce is barely at a simmer. Add the red pepper flakes, dried oregano, the dried onion powder, and sautéed mushrooms, and continue to simmer very gently over very low heat for 1 ½ hours stirring every few minutes making sure that the sauce does not burn. Towards the end of the simmering time, add the salt and pepper, tasting to see how much to add, and the sugar and taste to see if a little more is needed. Add the chopped parsley leaves, and stir.

Place a large pot of water on to boil. When it reaches a boil add the kosher salt and the pasta, return to a boil, and cook the linguine according to package directions until al dente (tender but firm to the bite). Remove 2 cups of sauce and place in a serving bowl. When the pasta is al dente remove it with a tongs and add it to the sauce. Toss with the tongs and place in a large serving bowl. Serve immediately. Place the bowl of reserved sauce on the table, along with a bowl of the grated Parmigiano-Reggiano on the table for everyone to help themselves.

This pasta can be served as a primi piatti (a first course) or as the main attraction. In true Italian style it would be served as a primi piatti. In my home it is often served as a main course. A salad with an olive oil vinaigrette such as Green Salad (page 164) goes beautifully with this pasta. The Toasted Garlic Bread on (page 7) also goes so well with this. The vegetable dish Simple Celery (page85) with a little parsley added is also a great dish to serve with this pasta. If you are serving this as a first course a great main course to serve with this is Roast Chicken (page 144). The pasta can be prepared while the chicken is roasting.

*To peel mushrooms - use a paring knife to remove the outer skin or layer of the mushroom.

Spaghetti with Tomato Meat Sauce

*Spaghetti con sugo di carne*

This is a favorite in my house. You can make a double recipe of the sauce and store the extra sauce for 2 or 3 days to be used on freshly cooked pasta. The sauce's flavors blend very well and is actually better the second day.

2 Tbsp. extra virgin olive oil

7 or 8 garlic cloves peeled and finely minced

1 large onion chopped

1 lb. extra lean ground beef *

½ tsp kosher salt

½ tsp. freshly ground black pepper

1 29 oz. (1 lb. 13 oz.) can tomato puree

1 6 oz. can tomato paste

1 bay leaf (remove before serving)

1 tsp. oregano or to taste

¼ tsp. onion powder or to taste (optional)

¼ tsp. garlic powder or to taste (optional)

¼ tsp. to ½ tsp. red pepper flakes or to taste (optional)

1 tsp. sugar or to taste (optional)

1/3 cup fresh parsley chopped

¼ cup fresh basil cut into a chiffonade instructions (page 25)

½ lb. (8 oz.) good quality dried spaghetti

1 Tbsp. kosher salt for the pasta cooking water

Freshly grated Parmigiano-Reggiano for sprinkling on individual servings at the table

In a large heavy bottomed pot heat the olive oil until it is hot enough to sizzle when a piece of garlic is placed in it. Add the garlic and stir with a wooden spoon, add the chopped onion and stir being careful not to let the garlic burn. When the onion is translucent and the garlic is starting to turn a light golden color, add the ground beef, when the beef starts to turn a light brown add the salt and pepper. Sauté until the ground beef has no pink left. Add the tomato puree and mix well. Turn down the heat so that the sauce comes to a low simmer. Stir very frequently to insure that the sauce does not burn. Add the tomato paste and thoroughly mix it into the sauce. Add the bay leaf, and oregano, and the optional red pepper flakes if they are desired. Simmer on very low heat for at least 45 minutes. Taste and adjust the seasonings. The optional onion and garlic powder could be added now if they are desired Simmer for another 45 minutes to 1 hour, and taste and adjust spices if necessary. If you wish to add the sugar, add it at this time.

Bring a large pot of water (4 to 5 quarts) on to boil. When it reaches a boil add 1 Tbsp. of kosher salt and the pasta and return to a boil. Cook the pasta according to package directions until al dente (tender but firm to the bite). While the pasta is boiling add the fresh parsley and basil to the tomato sauce. Remove the bay leaf. Ladle some of the sauce into a large sauté pan, and place over low heat. When the pasta is al dente, place it into the sauce using tongs. Toss thoroughly and place into a large warmed bowl. Serve with the freshly grated Parmigiano- Reggiano on the side.

Meatballs (page 50), served on the side is perfect with this.

*Use organic beef if possible. It is fairly quick and easy to make your own ground beef. If you do not have a meat grinder, you can put cubes of beef into your food processor and pulse until you reach the desired consistency.

Meatballs

*Polpettine*

1 Lb. extra lean ground beef*

1 medium onion cut into a small dice

1 egg slightly beaten

1 slice high quality white bread the crust removed

1/3 cup to ½ cup whole milk (enough to soften bread)

¾ cup chopped parsley

1 tsp. salt

¼ tsp. black pepper

extra virgin olive oil for sautéing

Tear the slice of bread onto pieces and place in a small bowl. Add the milk and thoroughly mush up the bread and milk with a fork. Add the slightly beaten egg, the salt and pepper, and mix together. Place the ground beef in a large bowl and add all of the rest of the ingredients to the ground beef. Mix together thoroughly. You can use a large spoon, but your hands make the best tools for this job. When the mixture is thoroughly combined form the meatballs. Make them small, about 1 inch in diameter.

Put enough olive oil in a large sauté pan to come up to a depth of ¼ inch. Heat the oil and when it is hot enough to sizzle when a small piece of the meatball mixture is placed in the oil, add the meatballs to the pan. Do not crowd. You may have to sauté the meatballs in batches. When the meatballs are nicely browned on all sides remove from your pan and drain on paper toweling, then place in a shallow baking dish and place in a 350 degree oven until the meatballs are cooked all the way through, with out any pink remaining in the centers. This will only take a few minutes. Lower the heat to 170 degrees F. and keep warm until you are ready to serve them.

These go very well with pasta and Marinara Sauce (page 44), or Spaghetti with Tomato Meat Sauce (page 47), or pasta with Fresh Tomato Sauce (page 42).

It is a personal preference of mine to always serve these on the side. You may add them to a tomato sauce if you wish.

These make a great antipasti also. Just be sure to keep them very small.

*Use organic beef if possible. It is fairly quick and easy to make your own ground beef. If you do not have a meat grinder, you can put cubes of beef into your food processor and pulse until you reach the desired consistency.

## Lasagne with Marinara Sauce

*Lasagne con sugo di pomodoro*

1 lb. (16 oz.) dried lasagne noodles

1 Tbsp.kosher salt for the pasta cooking water

3 ½ cups Marinara Sauce page 44

8 oz. mozzarella (sliced)

½ cup Parmigiano-Reggiano (grated)

1 cup ricotta cheese

extra virgin olive oil

Bring a large pot of water (4 to 5 quarts) to a boil. When it reaches a boil add the kosher salt and the pasta, return to a boil and prepare the lasagna noodles according to the package directions.

Place 1 cup of the marinara sauce into the baking dish. Top with a layer of lasagna noodles. Place ½ of the mozzarella slices over the noodles, and then sprinkle on ½ of the Parmigiano. Top this with ½ of the ricotta. Spread 1 cup of the marinara sauce over the ricotta. Place another layer of lasagna noodles over the sauce. Repeat the layering of the cheeses, and top this with 1 cup of sauce. Place remaining noodles over dish and spread the remaining ½ cup sauce over the noodles. Place in a preheated 350 degree oven for about 30 min. or until mixture is bubbling. Remove from oven and let stand 10 min. to set. Cut into squares to serve.

A salad with a vinaigrette, such as Green Salad (page 164) and toasted Italian Bread (page 20) or good quality Italian or French bread from the store is all you need to complete this meal.

Eggplant Lasagne

*Parmigiana di melanzane*

Enough eggplants to weigh approximately 24 oz.

3 ½ cups Marinara Sauce page 44

8 oz. mozzarella cut into slices

½ cup Parmigiano-Reggiano

1 cup ricotta cheese

extra virgin olive oil

Coat a rimmed baking sheet with olive oil and set aside. Peel eggplants and thinly slice crosswise. Place on the prepared baking sheet. Turn over so that the eggplant slices are coated with olive oil on both sides. Place in a pre-heated 375 degree F. oven for 10 to 15 minutes. Turn eggplant slices over and lower the heat to 350 degrees F. and bake for another 10 to 15 min. or until the slices are very soft. Place 1 cup of the marinara sauce into the baking dish. Top with a layer of eggplant slices, the slices can overlap slightly. Place ½ of the mozzarella slices on the dish and then sprinkle on ½ of the Parmigiano. Top with ½ of the ricotta. Top this with 1 ½ cups of the marinara sauce. Place another layer of eggplant slices on top of the sauce, and overlapping slightly is fine. Repeat the layering of the cheeses, and top with the remaining cup of marinara. Place in a preheated 350 degree Fahrenheit oven and bake for 1 ½ hours. Let cool for 20 minutes to set layers. Cut into squares and serve, with some finely grated Parmigiano the side.

Fusilli with Roasted Tomatoes

*Fusilli col pomodori al forno*

The tomatoes become so flavorful from roasting in the oven that they really do not need any salt or pepper. Once you have added the roasted tomatoes to the pasta, taste to see if you think the dish needs seasoning. The pepper flakes gives the dish a little extra liveliness, but is equally good without.

7 tomatoes garden fresh or supermarket vine-on tomatoes

extra virgin olive oil

1 tsp. peperoncini (red pepper flakes)

1 lb. package (16 oz.) of dried pasta, fusilli or penne

1 Tbsp. kosher salt for the pasta cooking water

Coat an oven-proof baking dish generously with olive oil. Cut a circle around the core at the stem-end of the tomatoes and remove core. You may peel the tomatoes, instructions for peeling page , or leave the skins on. Roughly chop the tomatoes and place in the baking dish. Bake in a 300 degree oven for 20 minutes, then turn tomatoes around, so that tomatoes are coated with the olive oil on all sides. Bake for an additional 20 to 25 minutes.

While the tomatoes are roasting,

Bring a large pot of water (4 to 5 quarts) on to boil. When it reaches a boil add the kosher salt and the pasta, return to a boil, and cook the pasta according to package directions until al dente (tender but firm to the bite). Remove the baking-dish with the tomatoes from the oven, and add the pasta to the tomatoes. Test to see if you wish to add salt and pepper at this time. You may add the peperoncini at this time also, if you wish.

Linguine and Peppers

*Linguine con peperoni*

extra virgin olive oil (enough to cover the bottom of a large sauté pan)

5 to 7 cloves of garlic peeled and finely chopped

3 peppers (1 orange pepper, 1 red pepper, 1 yellow pepper)

½ to 1 tsp. pepperincino (red pepper flakes) optional

salt and freshly ground pepper to taste

2 Tbsp. butter

1 lb. package (16 oz.) dried Linguine

1 Tbsp. kosher salt for the pasta water

2 cups grated Parmigiano-Reggiano

The peppers can be added raw or roasted to this dish. If you wish to roast them, place them in a pre-heated 350 degree F. oven. After 10 minutes, check them to see if their skins will peel off easily, if so remove from the oven and let cool until they are just warm and they are cool enough to handle. Remove the tops and bottoms and the cores including the seeds. Slice into ¼ inch strips.

Place a large pot of water(4 to 5 quarts) on to boil. When it reaches a boil add the kosher salt and the pasta, return to a boil, and cook according to the package directions until al dente (tender but firm to the bite).

Meanwhile as the water heats up, heat the olive oil over medium high heat in a sauté pan that is large enough to hold all of the pasta once it is cooked. Place the chopped garlic into the olive oil once it has reached the point that it sizzles when a piece of garlic is dropped into it. Sauté slightly, and add the pepperincino to taste if you are using it. If the peppers are roasted sauté the garlic until it is a light golden color before adding the peppers. Add the peppers, and sauté them until they are thoroughly cooked through and soft. Add the salt and pepper to taste. Add the butter to the pepper mixture. When the pasta is al dente add it to the sauté pan using a pair of tongs. Coat the pasta with the oil and butter and mix with the peppers. Adjust the salt, pepper and pepperincino to taste. Place in a serving dish and sprinkle with ½ cup of the grated Parmigiano cheese. Place the rest of the cheese in a separate dish, to be used as desired.

A salad with vinaigrette such as Green Salad (page164) goes very well with this. Toasted Garlic Bread (page 7) is also great with this pasta.

Fettuccine Tossed in Cream and Butter with Parmigiano

*Fettuccine In salsa bianca*

This is my version of a classic butter and cream sauce pasta. It is so easy and fast, yet so elegant. This is a great dish to prepare for guests especially if you do not have much time to prepare dinner.

1 lb package (16oz.) dried fettuccine

1 Tbsp. kosher salt for the pasta water

2/3 cup Parmigiano-Reggiano freshly grated for sauce and 1 cup freshly grated for serving at the table

¾ cup butter cut into 2 inch pieces

½ cup whipping cream (at room temperature)

salt and freshly ground pepper to taste

1 cup of the pasta cooking water

Place a large pot of water (4 to 5 quarts) on to boil. When it reaches a boil add the kosher salt and the pasta, return to a boil, and cook according to package directions until the pasta is al dente (tender but firm to the bite). Transfer the fettuccine with a large pair of tongs to a large sauté pan and add approximately 1/3 of the butter and 1/3 of the cream. Turn the heat on very low, just to keep the pasta warm. Gently toss until all of the butter and cream is incorporated. Repeat this process until all of the butter and cream is used. Add the salt and freshly ground pepper to taste. Add a Tbsp. or two of the reserved pasta water if the sauce is getting to thick. Add 1/3 cup of the cheese, and toss very lightly 2 or 3 times with the tongs or with 2 forks. Place the pasta in a large warm serving bowl. Sprinkle the rest of the cheese (1/3 cup) on top, and serve with ample additional cheese on the table for each person to add additional cheese to his or her serving.

A salad with olive oil and vinegar such as Green Salad (page164) goes well with this, as does Toasted Garlic Bread (page 7), and Asparagus with Olive Oil (page 73), makes a nice vegetable accompaniment.

Linguine with Prosciutto, Peas and Parmigiano

*Linguine con prosciutto e piselli al prosciutto*

This has been a favorite dish of my Grandson Evan since he was two years old. It is always so delightful to watch a young child enjoy food that is not only delicious but nutritious as well.

¼ cup extra virgin olive oil

5 cloves garlic

1 medium onion

8 very thin slices Prosciutto cut into 1 by 2 inch pieces

½ cup butter cut into 2 inch pieces

¾ cup cream (at room temperature)

1 package (10 oz.) frozen baby peas

1 cup freshly grated Parmigiano-Reggiano

kosher salt and freshly ground black pepper to taste

1 lb.package (16 oz.) dried linguine

1 Tbsp. kosher salt for the pasta cooking water

Bring a large pot of water (4 to 5 quarts) to boil. When it reaches a boil add the kosher salt and the pasta, return to a boil. Cook the pasta according to package directions until the pasta is al dente (tender but firm to the bite). While the pasta is cooking, place the baby peas in boiling salted water and simmer for 3 to 5 minutes. Heat the ¼ cup extra virgin olive oil in a large sauté pan and while the oil is heating peel the onion and chop it into a medium dice, peel and finely mince the garlic. Add the garlic when the oil is hot enough to sizzle when a piece of minced garlic is dropped into it, and gently sauté for a minute, then add the chopped onion. Watch carefully to make sure that the garlic turns only a golden color and the onion only becomes translucent and does not turn brown. Be very careful that you do not burn the garlic. When the onion is totally translucent and the garlic is starting to turn a light golden color, add the prosciutto, sauté for a few minutes, then add the baby peas. When the pasta is al dente transfer the linguine with tongs into the sauté pan and add the butter and the cream. Season with salt and pepper. Toss the pasta with your tongs until all the butter and cream are incorporated. Add the Parmigiano-Reggiano and toss very lightly. Place in a large bowl that has been warmed in the oven. Serve immediately with additional freshly grated Parmigiano-Reggiano.

Pasta in a Garlic Olive Oil and Butter Breadcrumb Sauce

*Spaghetti con briciolata*

½ cup extra virgin olive oil

½ cup butter

1 head of garlic peeled and finely chopped

1 cup of fresh breadcrumbs or dried crumbs (page 111)

a generous amount of freshly ground pepper to taste

1 lb. package (16 oz.) dry spaghetti or linguine

1 Tbsp. kosher salt for the pasta cooking water

freshly grated Parmigianino-Regianno for serving at the table

1 cup skillet dried breadcrumbs (page 112) for serving at the table

Place a large pot of water (4 to 5 quarts) on to boil. When it reaches a boil add the kosher salt and the pasta, return to a boil, and cook according to package directions until al dente (tender but firm to the bite). Meanwhile as the water heats up, heat the olive oil and the butter in a sauté pan large enough to hold all of the pasta once it is cooked. Place the finely chopped garlic into the olive oil and butter mixture once it has reached the point that it sizzles when a piece of garlic is added to it. Sauté the garlic until it is a light golden color, and then add the breadcrumbs. Stir the breadcrumbs and the chopped garlic in the oil and butter mixture and add the pepper. Stir the garlic and the breadcrumbs until they are a beautiful golden color. When the pasta is al-dente remove it from the water using a tongs and add it to the sauce. Toss the pasta together with the sauce using your tongs. Serve immediately with freshly grated Parmigianino Reggiano on the side.

Red Clam Sauce with Linguini

*Linguini con vongole*

½ cup water for cooking clams

2 dozen small littleneck or 3 dozen manila clams or 2 6 ½ oz. cans canned clams

1 tsp. extra virgin olive oil for sautéing mushrooms

8 oz. fresh mushrooms

4 or 5 Tbsp. extra virgin olive oil

3 or 4 garlic cloves peeled and finely minced

10 to 12 fresh tomatoes peeled and pureed or 3 cans 18 oz. each peeled Roma tomatoes pureed or 2 cans 28 oz. each tomato puree

½ tsp. dried oregano

1 tsp. fresh rosemary chopped

4 fresh leaves basil cut into a chiffonade instructions on page 25

¼ cup chopped fresh parsley (optional)

kosher salt and freshly ground black pepper to taste

1 lb. (16 oz.) good quality dried pasta

1 Tbsp. kosher salt for pasta water

For Fresh Clams

Fresh clams should be scrubbed with a brush under cold running water. Heat the ½ cup water and add the clams. Cover and cook over high heat for about 6 to 10 minutes shaking the pan occasionally until the clams open. Remove from the heat and uncover. Do not use any clams that have not opened after 10 minutes of cooking. Discard any unopened clams. Let the clams cool until they are cool enough to handle. Remove the clams from their shells over a bowl to catch their liquid. Strain the liquid through a sieve lined with cheesecloth or paper coffee filter to remove any sand that might remain. Reserve the strained liquid. Chop the clams into approximately ½ inch size pieces and reserve. Save the shells for decorating the serving plate.

For Canned Clams

If you are using canned clams, simply add them and their juices as described below.

Sauté the mushrooms in the 1 tsp. of olive oil until they are soft and aromatic. Reserve them to add to the sauce.

Heat the 4 to 5 Tbsp. olive oil in a large sauté pan. Add the garlic when the oil is hot enough to sizzle when a piece of minced garlic is dropped into it, and gently sauté, stirring and watching carefully so that the garlic does not burn. When the garlic is a light golden color add the tomato puree, the oregano, rosemary, the reserved clam juice from the fresh clams or the clam juice from the canned clams, (place the canned clams in a bowl and set aside), the reserved mushrooms and salt and black pepper to taste. Cook and stir for about 25 minutes.

While the sauce is simmering, Place a large pot of water (4 to 5 quarts) on to boil. When it reaches a boil add the 1 Tbsp. kosher salt and the pasta, return to a boil, and cook according to package directions until al dente (tender but firm to the bite).

When the pasta is about 5 minutes away from being done, add the reserved clams, or the canned clams, the fresh basil and parsley to the tomato sauce. When the pasta is al dente add it to the tomato sauce using a pair of tongs. If the sauce seems too thick add a little of the pasta cooking water and toss well for a minute or so to combine flavors.

Place the cooked pasta and sauce in a large serving bowl, if you used fresh clams, place the reserved shells around the edge of the serving bowl for decoration.

Green Beans with Butter (page 71) is a very nice vegetable to have with this dish.

Risotto with Mushrooms and Peas

*Risotto con fungi*

2 packages (8.oz.) white button mushrooms (peeled optional) instructionspage 44 rinsed and roughly chopped

1 cup small frozen or fresh peas

1/3 cup water for boiling the peas

2 Tablespoons extra virgin olive you may need a little more (enough to coat the bottom of a heavy bottomed pot)

½ cup chopped onion

1 ½ cups Arborio rice

7 cups homemade Brown Chicken Stock page 30 or 1 bouillon cube placed in a pot with 5 cups of cold water and brought to a boil

salt and freshly ground pepper to taste

3 Tbsp. butter

1/3 cup grated Parmigiano-Reggiano cheese

¼ cup chopped parsley

Place the cleaned and chopped mushrooms in a small pan, and place over medium heat. The water contained in the mushrooms themselves should be sufficient to cook them. Keep an eye on them as you are cooking the risotto and turn the heat off when they are cooked. Bring the peas to a boil, then reduce heat and simmer until done about 5 minutes and turn the heat off. Bring the chicken stock to a simmer, and keep it just barely simmering. Heat the olive oil in a large heavy bottomed pot until it is hot enough to sizzle when a piece of onion is placed in it. Add the chopped onion and stir with a wooden spoon. Sauté the onions, stirring frequently, until they are thoroughly translucent. Add the rice and stir to coat the rice with the olive oil. Sauté until the edges become translucent. Add a ladleful of chicken stock about 1/2 cup. If using homemade you may need to add salt at this time. Adjust the heat to a level that will keep the rice at a very gentle simmer. Never let the rice stick to the sides or the bottom of the pot. Cook stirring constantly, and add another ladleful when the stock has almost all been absorbed. Continue stirring and keep adding stock a ladleful at a time after it has been almost absorbed by the rice. It should take 15 to 20 minutes to cook. When the rice is close to being done, add the mushrooms, peas, and the chopped parsley, stirring to thoroughly mix in. When the rice is creamy but al dente, (you will need to taste to test for this), remove from the heat and beat in the butter until completely absorbed. Add the Parmigiano and beat it in also. Add the pepper to taste and add salt if needed. Serve at once and have additional grated Parmigiano available at the table.

# Side Dishes

## *Contorni*

## Artichokes with Melted Butter

*Carciofi col burro*

An artichoke set on the table makes any meal look festive. Young children love the ceremony of dipping the leaves into melted butter and scraping off the tender artichoke flesh with their teeth. My grandson Leighton was only 2 ½ when he was proudly showing me how to eat an artichoke.

1 globe artichoke

kosher salt for boiling the artichoke

2 Tbsp. melted butter per person

Bring a pot of water (large enough to hold the artichoke) to a boil and add the salt. Rinse the artichoke under running water with the top of the artichoke pointed up, so that the water will rinse away any sand or dirt that is between the leaves. Turn upside down to shake out the water. When artichokes are cut or trimmed they oxidize and turn dark rather quickly. To prevent this, rub the cut ends with a cut lemon. If you are preparing only 1 artichoke and you work quickly you will probably not need to rub lemon on the artichoke. Cut off the last ½ inch of the stem and discard. Cut the stem off at the base (so that it will stand upright) and reserve the stem. Cut off the tough outer green peel on the stem and discard. Reserve the light tender flesh of the inner stem. Peel off the 2 tough bottom rows of leaves and discard. Lay the artichoke on its side and cut off the top 1 ½ inches of leaves, so that the top is flat. Take a scissors and trim the points off of the rest of the leaves. Place the artichoke stem side down in the rapidly boiling water along with the reserved stem, and cover with an inverted heatproof lid to keep the artichoke submerged as much as possible. This helps to prevent discoloration. The lid should not completely cover the pot as you want some air over the artichoke. Artichokes may become bitter if covered completely when boiling. Boil for 35 to 45 minutes. The artichoke is done when the leaves pull out easily and the bottom is tender. Lift out of the water and place on a serving dish.

Give each person a small dish of melted butter to dip the artichoke leaves and heart into. If you have individual butter warmers, they make a nice presentation. I suggest that if children are being served that you omit the butter warmers, as you could easily have an accident with the candles. The butter can be melted in the kitchen and poured into individual dishes or ramekins. This is how my grandchildren eat and savor their artichokes. The traditional way to eat an artichoke is to pull off a leaf, dip it into melted butter and scrape off the tender flesh with your teeth. When all the leaves are gone you will have reached the heart. Remove the hairy choke (which is inedible) with the edge of a spoon, and you have come to the heart, the most prized part of the artichoke. Cut it into however many wedges as people you are serving, so that each person gets a piece.

## Broccoli with Olive Oil

*Broccoletti con olio d' oliva*

1 bunch broccoli

kosher salt

sea salt and freshly ground pepper

extra virgin olive oil for serving at the table

Rinse the broccoli under cold running water. Cut off the bottom, you may use the first 4 to 6 inches of the main stalk closest to the florets, if you wish. If you choose to use the main stalk, peel it and cut it into pieces of an inch long.

Bring a small amount of water to boil in a sauce pot. The water should come up about an inch on the bottom of the pot. When the water comes to a boil add the kosher salt and then the broccoli. The water should not cover the broccoli. Cover and return to a boil and then reduce the heat to a simmer. Watch them and add a little more water if need be.

Remove the broccoli when they are fork tender and place on a serving dish. Drizzle with olive oil and serve as soon as possible. Place sea salt and freshly ground pepper along with extra olive oil on the table for your family and guests to serve themselves.

## Green Beans with Butter

*Fagiolini verdi col burro*

1 lb. tender green beans

kosher salt

1 ½ Tbsp. butter

sea salt and freshly ground pepper to taste

Snap off the ends of each bean and pull the attached string along the side of the bean to remove it. Rinse under cold water.

Add enough water to a skillet to have a depth of about ½ inch. Bring the water to a boil. Add the kosher salt and then the beans. Cover and return to a boil. Reduce the heat to a low simmer. Watch the beans very closely to make sure the water does not boil away. Add a little more water as necessary. Cook 7 to 10 minutes until the beans are just tender. If there is much water left in the pan remove it. Add the butter and toss thoroughly with the butter. Add the sea salt and freshly ground pepper to taste and serve while still hot.

This should serve 4

Sautéed Spinach

*Spinaci saltati*

This recipe exemplifies Tuscan cuisine to me. It is simple, nutritious and elegant.

1 bunch spinach rinsed thoroughly (stems and any thick veins removed)

extra virgin olive oil enough to coat the bottom of your saucepan very lightly (around 2 tsp)

¼ cup golden raisins

walnuts or Toasted Walnuts recipe page 117, or Toasted Pine Nuts page 118

sea salt and freshly ground pepper for serving at the table

2 lemons each cut in half crosswise

In a medium size saucepan heat the olive oil until it is hot enough to sizzle when a spinach leaf is added to it. Add the spinach. You will not need to add any water. The water in the spinach itself and the water clinging to the leaves from rinsing them will be enough. Stir and turn down the heat and continue to cook stirring occasionally. Add the golden raisins and continue to cook until the spinach is thoroughly wilted and cooked down. Add the walnuts or pine nuts.

Remove from the heat and serve with a half of a lemon for each person.

Serves 4

## Asparagus with Olive Oil

*Asparagi con olio d' oliva*

I make this dish as often as I can when asparagus are in season. It is a shame that the season is so short. It seems everyone has vegetables that they like and do not like, but it seems that everyone loves asparagus.

1 bunch fresh asparagus

kosher salt

sea salt and freshly ground pepper for serving at the table

extra virgin olive oil for serving at the table

Thoroughly rinse asparagus stalks and break off the tough bottom third or half if need be. You want only the tender upper part of the asparagus.

Bring a small amount of water to a boil in a saucepan. The water should reach a depth of about an inch on the bottom of the saucepan. Add the kosher salt and then the asparagus. The water should not cover the asparagus. Cover the pot and return to a boil. Reduce the heat to a simmer and cook until the asparagus stalks are tender. Watch them closely and add a little more water if need be.

Remove the asparagus from the water and place on n ovenproof serving dish that has been warmed in a 150 degree Fahrenheit oven.

Drizzle with olive oil and serve immediately. Place sea salt and freshly ground pepper along with additional olive oil on the table for your family and guests to serve themselves.

## Green Tomatoes Fried in Olive Oil

*Pomodori fritti*

These are fairly hard to find in most grocery stores, but if you grow your own tomatoes try picking a few tomatoes when they are not yet ripened and still green. It is definitely worth growing some homegrown tomatoes in order to enjoy this dish. You may be able to find green tomatoes at some farmers markets.

3 medium sized green tomatoes

flour for dredging

salt and freshly ground black pepper to taste

extra virgin olive oil (enough to cover the bottom of your sauté-pan with ¼ inch of oil)

Place the flour in a bowl, and season the flour with the salt and pepper. Cut the stem end off of the tomatoes and slice them into approximately ¼ inch slices. Heat the olive oil in a large sauté pan or skillet until it is hot enough to sizzle when a piece of tomato is added to it. Dredge the tomato slices in the seasoned flour mixture and shake off the excess. Place the slices into the hot olive oil. Sauté the tomato slices gently on both sides, and drain them on a paper toweling lined plate or sheet pan. Transfer to an oven proof serving platter and keep warm until you are ready to serve them.

They go very nicely with Toasted Garlic Bread - Fettunta (page7)

Golden Eggplant Slices

*Melanzane 'indorate'*

2 Asian (slender) or small globe eggplants about ¾ to 1 lb.

1 cup unbleached all-purpose flour

salt & freshly ground pepper

olive oil (enough to cover the bottom of a large sauté pan or skillet to a depth of ¼ to ½ inch)

Peel and slice eggplants into 3/8 inch slices. Combine the flour, salt and pepper in a large bowl. In a large sauté pan or skillet heat the olive oil until it is hot enough to sizzle when a piece of eggplant is added to it. Place the eggplant slices into the seasoned flour and shake off the excess. Place the slices into the hot oil. Do not crowd. Turn over with a metal spatula when the bottom turns a nice deep golden brown (around 4 to 7 minutes). Fry on the other side another 4 to 7 minutes, or until both sides are a beautiful deep golden brown, and the insides are thoroughly cooked through. With you spatula remove the slices and place on a paper toweling lined plate to drain. Fry the rest of the eggplant slices the same way. Place on paper toweling to drain and transfer to an ovenproof platter and keep warm until you are ready to serve them.

Serves 4

Eggplant Lasagne

*Timballo di melanze*

eggplants (approximately 24 oz.)

3 ½ cups Marinara Sauce (page44)

8 oz. mozzarella

½ cup Parmigiano -Reggiano

1 cup ricotta cheese

extra virgin olive oil

Coat a rimmed baking sheet with olive oil and set aside. Peel eggplants and thinly slice crosswise. Place on the prepared baking sheet. Turn over so that the eggplant slices are coated with olive oil on both sides. Place in a pre-heated 375 degree Fahrenheit oven for 10 to 15 minutes. Turn eggplant slices over and lower the heat to 350 degrees and bake for another 10 to 15 min or until the slices are very soft. Remove from the oven and set aside. Place 1 cup of the marinara sauce into the baking dish. Top with a layer of eggplant slices, the slices can overlap slightly. Place ½ of the mozzarella slices on the dish and then sprinkle ½ of the Parmigiano. Top with ½ of the ricotta. Top this with 1 ½ cups of the marinara sauce. Place another layer of eggplant slices on top of the sauce, and overlapping slightly is fine. Repeat the layering of the cheeses, and top with the remaining cup of marinara. Place in a preheated 350 degree oven and bake for 1 ½ hours. Let cool for 20 minutes to set layers. Cut into squares and serve, with some finely grated Parmigiano on the side.

## Carrots Roasted with Olive Oil

*Carote arrosta*

5 or 6 medium size carrots

2 tsp. extra virgin olive oil

2 tsp. water

pinch of kosher salt

Cut off the top end of the carrots and the very pointy bottoms. Peel and rinse off the carrots. Slice into ¼ inch slices. Place into a shallow dish such as a glass pie plate or other oven proof glass or porcelain dish. Drizzle the olive oil and water over the carrots, making sure that they are coated with the oil on all sides. Add a little more oil if necessary to coat. Sprinkle a little salt on the carrots, and place in a preheated 350 degree Fahrenheit oven for 15 to 25 min.

Brussels Sprouts Roasted in Olive Oil

*Cavolini di bruxelles arrosto*

Brussels sprouts roasted in this manner get a rich flavor from the olive oil and the caramelizing process. I love brussel s sprouts and this is one of my favorite ways to prepare them. My whole family enjoys brussels sprouts roasted like this, even those who are not particularly fond of brussel s sprouts.

20 to 25 brussels sprouts

1 Tbsp. water

2 Tbsp. extra virgin olive oil

kosher salt and freshly ground pepper to taste

Take off the outer leaves of the brussels sprouts if they are damaged. Cut off the stem ends if they look old, rinse in cold water, then cut each sprout in half. Put the water and olive oil in an oven-proof sauté pan or skillet with a lid. Place the sprouts cut side down in the pan, season them with salt and pepper, then cover with a lid. Heat the sprouts over medium high heat. When the water starts to bubble, turn down the heat to a bare simmer. Watch carefully to make sure that the sprouts do not start to burn. Add a little additional water if necessary. Cook for 5 minutes. Remove the lid and place in a preheated 350 degree Fahrenheit oven. Roast for 20 to 25 minutes. They are done when the outer leaves are caramelized and the centers of the sprouts are tender when pierced with a fork or the tip of a knife.

## Brussels Sprouts in Parchment Packages

*Cavolini de bruxelles in cartoccio*

This recipe is almost the same as the previous recipe, except that there is no pan to clean afterwards.

10 to 15 brussels sprouts

1 Tbsp. extra virgin olive oil

approximately 2 tsp. water

kosher salt and freshly ground pepper to taste

Take off outer leaves of the brussels sprouts if they are damaged. Cut off the stem ends of the sprouts if they look old, then cut each sprout in half. Lay a sheet of tin foil down and spread a layer of parchment paper over the foil. Place the sprouts on the parchment paper, and season the sprouts with salt and pepper to taste. Gather the foil and parchment paper into a pouch. Leave the pouch open enough so that you can pour the olive oil and the water into the pouch. Stir the sprouts around in the oil with your fingers to coat all sides of the sprouts with the oil. Pinch the pouch together at the top, leaving an opening at the top of about 1 inch. Place in a preheated 350 degree Fahrenheit oven. The outer leaves should start to caramelize in about 25 minutes. Check on them at this point and pierce one to see if it is tender, if it is not let them roast another 5 to 10 minutes. They should be done in about 25 to 35 minutes.

Serves 2

Simple Brussels Sprouts

*Cavolini de bruxelles*

30 fairly small brussels sprouts

kosher salt

salt and freshly ground pepper to taste

extra virgin olive oil for serving at the table

Remove the outer leaves of the sprouts and cut off the ends off the sprouts if the look old. Rinse in cold water. Bring a medium sized pot of water to a boil. There should be enough water to just cover them. Add the kosher salt and then the sprouts. Cover and return to a boil. Then lower the heat and simmer until tender. Remove from the water and serve with a good quality extra virgin oil, along with salt and pepper at the table for each person to season their sprouts.

Serves 4 to 5

Fried Zucchini Flowers and Zucchini Slices

*Fiorii di zucca fritti*

My Grandmother Rosalie brought zucchini seeds with her when she came to the United States from Tuscany. She made fried zucchini flowers from the zucchini that she grew in her garden. Zucchini has a place in my garden every year for the precious zucchini flowers. The fried flowers are an annual treat at my house. They should be picked on the morning that the blossoms open. The zucchini blossoms are very fragile, so place the stems in a glass of water, and store in the refrigerator, if you are not going to use them right away. They will keep a day or so that way. They can be hard to find in the stores, you may be able to find them at your local farmers market. If you do not have zucchini flowers, the zucchini slices prepared in this manner are also very delicious.

4 or 5 Zucchini flowers

2 small zucchini (about 6 to 8 inches long) peeled and sliced. The slices should be about ¼ to 1/3 inch thick

1 egg

1 to 2 tsp. sparkling water

1 cup flour

salt and white pepper to taste

extra virgin olive oil (enough to cover the bottom of a large sauté pan or skillet to a depth of ¼ inch.)

Rinse off the zucchini flowers very gently, they can be damaged easily. Remove the pistil (the thick center stem) from the inside of the flowers.

Beat the egg with the sparkling water in a bowl large enough to dip the zucchini flowers, and the zucchini into the egg mixture. In a separate bowl also large enough to hold the flowers and zucchini mix the flour with the salt and pepper. Heat the olive oil in a sauté pan or a skillet over medium heat. Place the zucchini flowers and the slices into the seasoned flour and shake off the excess flour. Then dip the flowers and slices into the egg mixture, remove and let the excess egg mixture drip off. They should have just a light coating. When the oil is hot enough to sizzle when a piece of zucchini is dropped into it, place the zucchini slices and zucchini flowers in the sauté pan. Do not crowd, you may have to sauté in 2 batches. Turn over with a set of tongs or a fork when the bottom side turns a nice golden brown. Lift out of the oil when both sides are a beautiful golden brown. Drain and pat dry in paper towels. Place on an oven proof serving dish and keep in a 250 degree Fahrenheit oven until ready to serve. Serve as quickly as possible or keep very hot in the oven.

Serves 4

Celery Fried in Olive Oil

*Sadano fritte*

5 or 6 celery stalks (organic if possible)

water for parboiling the celery

kosher salt for parboiling

1 Tbsp. sparkling water

1 cup of flour

salt and white pepper to taste

1 large egg

extra virgin olive oil (enough to cover the bottom of a large sauté pan or skillet to a depth of about ¼ inch).

Cut off the bottom of the celery and cut off the tips of the celery by about ¼ of an inch, if the tips are dried out. Thoroughly rinse off the celery to remove any dirt Remove any tough strings from the stalks by placing your knife under the strings and pulling them lengthwise down the celery stalk. Or remove the strings with a vegetable peeler by shaving a thin layer off. Cut the stalks into pieces about 1 ½ inches long.

Bring enough water to cover the celery in a pan deep enough to hold all of the celery at once. When the water comes to a boil, add the kosher salt, then add the celery pieces. Cover and let the water come back to a boil. Boil the celery for 1 to 2 minutes. Remove from the water and let the celery cool. While the celery is cooling, mix the flour with the salt and white pepper in a bowl large enough to hold the celery pieces. In a separate bowl of similar size beat the egg with the sparkling water.

When the celery is cool enough to handle place them into the seasoned flour mixture and coat on all sides, then dip into the beaten egg mixture.

Gently place the coated celery into a sauté pan with olive oil that has been heated to the point that it sizzles when a piece of celery is dropped into it. Turn the celery over with tongs or a fork when the bottom side turns a nice golden brown. Remove from the oil when both sides are a beautiful golden brown. Place on a plate lined with paper toweling to remove excess oil, then place in an oven proof serving dish and place in a warm oven until ready to serve. Serve as quickly as possible or keep warm in the oven.

Serves 4

Simple Celery

*Sedano*

1 bunch celery (organic if possible)

2 tsp. kosher salt

¼ cup chopped parsley (optional)

Cut off the bottom of the celery and cut off the tips by about ¼ of an inch, if the tips are dried out. Remove all leaves and reserve for another use. Thoroughly rinse off the celery to remove any dirt. Remove all tough strings from the stalks by placing your knife under the strings and pulling them lengthwise down the celery stalk. Or remove the strings with a vegetable peeler by shaving a thin layer off. Cut stalks into 1 inch pieces. Place in salted boiling water, (there should be enough water to cover the celery). Cover and reduce to a simmer. Cook until the celery is tender about 5 to 10 min. If you are using the optional parsley add it to the celery in the last 2 minutes of cooking.

Serves 6

Gratin of Celery with Béchamel

*Sedano gratinato con balsamella*

1 cup Béchamel Sauce(Balsamella) page 119

2 bunches celery (organic if possible) to equal about 2 cups chopped celery

2 tsp. kosher salt for boiling the celery

4 Tbsp. Breadcrumbs page 111

3 Tbsp. melted butter

Prepare the Béchamel (Balsamella) on page 119

Cut off the bottom of the celery and cut off the tips by about ¼ of an inch, if the tips are dried out. Remove all leaves and reserve for another use. Thoroughly rinse off the celery to remove any dirt. Remove all tough strings from the stalks by placing your knife under the strings and pulling them lengthwise down the celery stalk. Or remove the strings with a vegetable peeler by shaving a thin layer off. Cut stalks into 1 inch pieces. Place in salted boiling water, (there should be enough water to cover the celery). Cover and return to a boil and then reduce to a simmer. Cook until the celery is tender about 5 to 10 min. Spread ½ cup of the Balsamella sauce in an oven proof dish. The sauce should just thinly coat the bottom of the dish. Remove the celery from the water with a slotted spoon or strainer, and place on top of the Balsamella sauce in your oven proof dish. Sprinkle the bread crumbs over the sauce, then drizzle the melted butter over the top. Place in a preheated 350 degree Fahrenheit oven and bake until the bread crumbs are golden brown. Serve while still hot.

## Buttered Leeks

*Porri al burro*

This is elegant, simple and delicious.

4 leeks

4 Tbsp. butter

1/2 cup water

salt and freshly ground pepper to taste

½ cup Buttered Breadcrumbs page 112

Cut off the root ends and the dark green tops of the leeks. Slice in half lengthwise, and rinse under cold running water to remove any dirt or sand. Cut the leeks into julienne strips about 1/4 inch by 3 inches. Place the water and butter into a pan, and bring to a simmer. Add the leeks, and simmer until the leeks are tender. You may have to add a little additional water. Add salt and pepper and place in a serving dish and top with the buttered breadcrumbs. Serve immediately, or place in a warm oven until you are ready to serve.

This goes well as a side for Leg of Lamb with Roasted Potatoes (page 133),Standing Rib Roast with Roasted Potatoes (page 124), Roast Chicken (Page 144), or any roasted meat.

Roasted Garlic

*Aglio arrosto*

My daughte -in-law, Molly has perfected this. It is so delicious! I first had Molly's version of this when she and my son had the family over for Christmas dinner.

2 Tbsp. butter

1 head of garlic

Melt the butter in an ovenproof glass dish such as a Pyrex muffin cup in a 350 degree Fahrenheit oven. Slice the bottom off of the garlic head and place in the glass dish with the butter. Roast in the oven for 45 minutes. Watch the garlic to make sure there is still butter in the dish. If the butter has been absorbed by the garlic, add more butter. When the garlic is starting to turn golden, remove from the oven. The garlic should be soft and have a rich and mellow garlicky taste,

This can be served with Standing Rib Roast with Roasted Potatoes (page 124), or Leg of Lamb with Roasted Potatoes (page 133) or any roasted meat.

## Tomatoes and Zucchini

*Pomodori di zucchini saltate*

2 Tbsp. extra virgin olive oil (enough to coat the bottom of a medium sauté pan)

4 ripe plum tomatoes, or 2 medium beefsteak tomatoes, or 2 vine on tomatoes, or 2 medium tomatoes of a similar type

3 or 4 small zucchinis

4 sprigs curly leaf parsley finely chopped (optional)

salt & freshly ground pepper to taste

Cut the stem ends off the tomatoes, then the tomatoes can be used either peeled or unpeeled, instructions for peeling tomatoes are on page 136. Next slice the tomatoes in half, and cut those halves into approximately 1 inch chunks. Cut the tops off the zucchinis, and a small slice off the other end. Slice the zucchinis into ¼ inch thick slices.

Heat your sauté pan with the olive oil over medium heat until it is hot enough to sizzle when a piece of tomato is added to the oil. Then add the rest of the tomato. Cook the tomato for a few minutes, until it begins to soften, and then add the zucchinis. Add the salt and the freshly ground pepper to taste. If you are adding the parsley add it now. Stir frequently over medium heat until the vegetables are fork tender. Place in a serving dish and keep warm until served.

Celery with Tomatoes

*Sedano con pomodori*

2 Tbsp. extra virgin live oil or enough to coat the bottom of a medium sauté-pan

5 celery stalks (organic if possible)

4 ripe plum tomatoes, or 2 medium beefsteak tomatoes, or 2 medium tomatoes of a similar type

4 sprigs curly leaf parsley with the stems removed, finely chopped (optional)

salt & freshly ground pepper to taste

Cut the stem ends off the tomatoes, then the tomatoes can be used either peeled or unpeeled. Instructions for peeling tomatoes are on page 136. Next slice the tomatoes in half, then cut those halves into approximately 1 inch chunks.

Cut the leaves off the celery and use them for something else. Cut off the bottom ends of the celery stalks and cut off the top ends of the celery by about ¼ of an inch, if the ends are dried out. Cut off all the leaves and save them for something else. Thoroughly rinse off the celery to remove any dirt Remove any tough strings from the stalks by placing your knife under the strings and pulling them lengthwise down the celery stalk, or remove the strings with a vegetable peeler by shaving a thin layer off. Slice the stalks into ¼ to 1/3 inch slices. Heat the olive oil in your sauté-pan. Add the tomato pieces to the olive oil when it is hot enough to sizzle when a piece of tomato is dropped into the oil. Cook the tomato for a few minutes, and then add the celery. Add the salt and the freshly ground pepper. If you are adding the parsley, add it now. Stir frequently over medium heat until the vegetables are fork tender. Place in a serving dish and keep warm until served.

Zucchini and Celery with Tomatoes

*Zucchine di sedano con pomodori*

2 Tbsp. olive oil (or enough to coat the bottom of a medium sauté pan)

4 small zucchini's

4 stalks celery

4 ripe plum tomatoes or 2 medium beefsteak tomatoes, or a similar type of tomato

4 sprigs of curly leaf parsley (optional)

salt & freshly ground pepper to taste

Cut off the tops of the tomatoes and slice the tomatoes in half, then cut those halves into approximately 1 inch chunks.

Cut off the bottom ends of the celery stalks and cut off the top ends of the celery by about ¼ of an inch, if the ends are dried out. Cut off all the leaves and save them for something else. Thoroughly rinse off the celery to remove any dirt. Remove any tough strings from the stalks by placing your knife under the strings and pulling them lengthwise down the celery stalk, or remove the strings with a vegetable peeler by shaving a thin layer off. Slice into ½ inch slices. Heat the olive oil in a sauté pan. Place the tomato pieces into the olive oil once it has reached the point that it sizzles when a piece of tomato is dropped into it. Sauté the tomato for a few minutes and then add the celery. Sauté for a few minutes, and then add the zucchini. Add the salt and freshly ground pepper. If you are adding parsley, add it now. Stir frequently on medium heat until the vegetables are fork tender. Place in a serving dish and keep warm until served.

This goes very nicely with Roast Chicken (page 144) or with Chickpea Patties (page 104. It also makes a very nice dish for lunch served with Scrambled Eggs with Gruyère Cheese (page 152), and Italian Bread (page 20) or purchased Italian or French bread, or for a light lunch serve this with just the bread.

## Zucchini and Tomato Gratin

*Pomodori gratinati*

1/8 cup extra virgin olive oil (approximately) for oiling baking dish

4 medium zucchini

2 medium tomatoes

1/8 cup extra-virgin olive oil

4 leaves of fresh basil cut into a chiffonade (optional) directions for chiffonade on page 25

¼ cup finely chopped curly leaf parsley

salt and freshly ground black pepper to taste

½ cup fresh breadcrumbs page 111

Oil a baking dish that has low sides (about 1 ½ to 2 ½ inchs) such as a pie plate or an ovenproof ceramic or porcelain baking dish. Cut the ends off of the zucchini. The zucchini may be used peeled or unpeeled whichever you wish. Cut into ¼ inch thick slices and place half of the slices in the baking dish. Salt and pepper the slices. Core the tomatoes and peel them. Instructions for peeling tomatoes on page 136. Slice the tomatoes into ¼ inch slices and place them over the zucchini slices. Salt and pepper the tomato slices and place the remainder of the zucchini slices on top of the tomato layer. Salt and pepper the last layer of zucchini slices. If you are using the chiffonade of basil spread it over the zucchini slices. Sprinkle generously with the breadcrumbs. Place into a pre-heated 350 degree Fahrenheit oven. Bake for 30 to 40 minutes until the vegetables are cooked through and tender and the top is golden and crisp.

## Potatoes Roasted with Olive Oil

*Patate al forno e olio d' oliva*

3 medium size russet potatoes

extra virgin olive oil

salt to taste

Peel the potatoes and slice them very thinly. Cut the slices in half and if the potatoes are very large in girth cut the slices in half again. Coat an oven-proof dish with olive oil and toss the sliced potatoes in the oil to coat them. Spread them out in a single layer. Sprinkle with a little salt to taste and place in a preheated 350 degree Fahrenheit oven. Check on them after 10 to 12 minutes, they may take a little longer, 15 minutes or so, depending on the size of the slices. They are done when they are tender in the center and crispy and brown on the outer edges. Serve while still hot.

Serves 4

## Oven Crisped Potatoes

*Patate al forno*

These can be made quite quickly. I often get requests for these as a side dish. They get crisp on the outside and very tender and soft on the inside.

5 russet potatoes

extra virgin olive oil (enough to coat a shallow baking dish)

salt and freshly ground black pepper

Generously coat an oven-proof baking dish such as an 8 by 12 inch glass or porcelain dish with olive oil. Peel and chop the potatoes into a ½ inch dice. Fill the baking dish with the diced potatoes. They should completely fill the baking dish in just a single layer. Roll the potato pieces around in the olive oil until they are covered with olive oil on all sides. Place in a preheated 350 degree Fahrenheit oven. Check on the potatoes after 15 minutes, if they are golden brown on the bottom, take a metal spatula and scrape the bottom of the baking dish to get all the crispy bits lifted up. Turn the potatoes over and let them turn golden brown on the other side. You may want to do this one more time. Remove from the oven, and serve while still hot.

Serves 4

## Potato Gratin

*Patate gratinate*

Here is one of my Mother Marguerite's potato recipes. It has a delicate rich flavor. You need to be astute enough to enrich the potatoes without making it too rich and masking the delicate flavor of the dish.

5 russet potatoes

3 tsp. butter (divided)

salt and white pepper to taste

whole milk

1 ½ quart soufflé dish or other casserole dish with high sides

Peel and cut the potatoes into thin slices. Place a few small dots of butter (about 1 tsp.) on the bottom of your soufflé dish. Place a layer of potato slices to cover the bottom of the dish. Lightly salt and pepper the potato layer, and sprinkle ½ tsp. of the flour over the potatoes. Place a few small dots of butter (½ to1 tsp.) spaced out evenly over the potato layer.

Repeat the layering process until the casserole dish is 2/3 filled. Lightly salt and pepper the dish and it is ready to have the milk poured in. Pour enough milk to come up to the top layer but not over it. Do not let the milk cover the top. Place a few small dots of butter on top.

Place in a 350 degree Fahrenheit preheated oven. Bake for 1 to 1 ½ hours. The top should become a beautiful golden brown. Remove from the oven and let sit for at least 15 minutes before serving. It needs to cool down a little and firm up.

Serves 6

Potatoes Crisped with Butter

*Patate con burro*

I like to serve these with leftover cold turkey or chicken. This is a side dish that we have the day after Thanksgiving with turkey. This is rich and delicious.

¼ Lb. butter

4 to 5 russet potatoes

¼ cup finely chopped chives (optional)

salt and freshly ground pepper

Melt the butter in a large sauté pan. Peel and chop the potatoes into a fine dice ¼ to 1/3 inch. Add the diced potatoes to the butter when it is hot enough to sizzle when a piece of potato is dropped into it. Let the potatoes sauté until they are golden brown and crisp on the bottom. With a metal spatula, scrape up all the golden brown potato bits and turn over. Let turn golden brown on the bottom and repeat the scraping and turning. You may need to add more butter as the potatoes cook if they are starting to dry out. Keep sautéing the potatoes until they are a beautiful golden brown on all sides, and crisped on the outside and cooked through on the inside. Add the finely chopped chives if you are using them during the last minute or so of sautéing. Season with salt and freshly ground pepper to taste.

Serves 4

Mashed Potatoes with Leeks Sautéed in Olive Oil

*Pure di patate cremoso*

The sautéed leeks are a great addition and give a subtle flavor to the potatoes. The sautéed leeks can be omitted if you wish and you will have excellent plain mashed potatoes.

7 or 8 russet potatoes  peeled and cut into thirds

2 tsp. kosher salt

2 to 3 Tbsp. butter

3 Tbsp. whole milk or cream or enough to keep the potatoes fluffy

For leeks

1 to 2 Tbsp. extra virgin olive oil (enough to coat your sauté pan)

2 medium leeks

Place cold water in a large pot and bring it to a boil. While the water is heating peel and cut the potatoes into large chunks. When the water reaches a boil add the kosher salt, and then the potatoes. Partially cover the pot and bring back to a boil. Reduce the heat and let the potatoes cook at a low boil. Cook until the potatoes are tender about 20 to 30 minutes depending on the size of the chunks of potato.

While potatoes are boiling, prepare the leeks. Cut off the root ends and the dark green tops. Make a slit running lengthwise to the center of the leeks from the top to the bottom, so that you can open up the leeks and rinse them under cold running water to remove any dirt or sand. Chop the leeks into a ¼ inch dice. Heat the olive oil in a sauté pan until it is hot enough to sizzle when a piece of leek is dropped into it. Place the chopped leeks into the olive oil and sauté until the leeks are soft and translucent.

The potatoes are done when they can be easily pierced with a fork. Drain the potatoes reserving ½ cup of the cooking water in case the potatoes are too dry. Pass the potatoes through a potato ricer back into the pot that you boiled them in. Place over very low heat making sure that they do not burn. Add 2 to 3 Tbsp. butter and enough whole milk or cream, (added a little at a time) until thoroughly incorporated to make the potatoes fluffy and smooth. If they seem too dry add as much as needed of the reserved cooking water. Add the sautéed leeks. Serve immediately or place in an oven proof serving dish and keep them warm in the oven until you are ready to serve them.

## Potato Croquettes

*Croccette di papate*

I have made these since I was 12. They were my specialty and on holidays I made them for the antipasti course. They make a great side dish also.

5 russet potatoes

2 tsp. salt for boiling potatoes

3 Tbsp. butter

2 to 3 Tbsp. whipping cream or whole milk

2 eggs

unbleached all-purpose flour for dredging

butter for sautéing (enough to cover the bottom of a large sauté pan or skillet to a depth of ¼ inch)

Place cold water in a large pot and bring it to a boil. While the water is heating peel and cut the potatoes into large chunks. When the water reaches a boil, add the kosher salt and then the potatoes. Partially cover the pot and bring back to a boil. Reduce the heat and let the potatoes cook at a low boil. Cook until the potatoes are tender, about 20 to 30 minutes depending on the size of the chunks of potato. The potatoes are done when they can be easily pierced with a fork. Drain the potatoes reserving ½ cup of the cooking water in case the potatoes are too dry. Pass the potatoes through a potato ricer, back into the pot that you boiled them in. Place over very low heat making sure that they do not burn. Mix in the butter, and the whole milk or cream (added a little at a time) until thoroughly incorporated, to make the potatoes fluffy and smooth. If they seem too dry add as much as needed of the reserved cooking water. Remove from the heat and add the salt and white pepper to taste.

Lightly beat one of the eggs and add it to the potato mixture. Set aside until you are ready to sauté them.

Beat the remaining egg in a bowl. Place the flour in a separate bowl. Form the potatoes into croquettes using about 1 ½ Tbsp. for each. They should be about 1 ½ to 2 inches long and cylindrical in shape. Heat the butter in a large sauté pan over medium heat. Place each croquette in the flour and coat on all sides. Next place each croquette into the beaten egg, and coat on all sides.

When the butter is hot enough to sizzle when a small piece of potato mixture is dropped into it, place the croquettes into the sauté pan. Sauté until the croquettes are a beautiful golden brown on the bottom. Turn over as necessary with a metal spatula scraping up any browned bits until they are golden brown all over.

Remove from the butter and place on a plate lined with paper toweling to drain and cool a little. Serve them, or place on an oven proof platter and keep them warm in the oven.

Cannellini Beans Drizzled with Olive Oil

*Fagioli bolliti*

Tuscans have long been called mangia fagioli or bean eaters. No wonder since beans are so nutritious and economical. My Grandmother Rosalie prepared cannellini beans in this delicious and simple way. She always used dried beans, but if you are pressed for time the canned beans can make a quick and delicious dish.

2/3 cup dried cannellini beans or 1 15 oz. can cannellini beans (preferably organic)

1 tsp. chopped fresh rosemary or 2 Tbsp. finely chopped curly parsley

extra virgin olive oil for drizzling

1 lemon cut into wedges for squeezing over beans

sea salt and freshly ground pepper to taste

For dried beans:

Pick through and discard any stones or damaged beans, and rinse thoroughly.

For the quick soak method: Place the beans in a large pot and cover with cold water. Bring to a boil and boil for 2 to 3 minutes. Turn off the heat, and cover the pot and let sit for 1 to 4 hours.

For the long soak method: Place the beans in a large bowl or pot, and cover with cold water and let sit for 8 to 12 hours.

After using either soaking method drain and rinse the beans. Place in a pot and cover with cold water (3 parts water to 1 part beans). Bring to a boil and boil without a cover for 10 minutes. Place a lid on the pot and reduce the heat and simmer until tender, 1 to 3 hours. The beans are tender when you can squash them between your tongue and palate. Add the rosemary or parsley during the last 10 minutes of cooking.

For canned beans:

Drain the beans and rinse them under cold water. Place in a pot and heat. Add the rosemary or parsley.

After cooking either dried or canned beans, add the sea salt and pepper at this time. Serve with olive oil for drizzling and lemon wedges.

Cannellini Beans with Sage Olive Oil

*Cannellini con olio d' olive e salvia*

2/3 cup dried cannellini beans or 1 15 oz. can cannellini beans (preferably organic)

10 to 15 fresh sage leaves

½ cup extra virgin olive oil

sea salt and freshly ground pepper to taste

For the dried beans:

Follow the directions for soaking and cooking the beans on page 101.

For canned beans:

Drain the beans and rinse them under cold water. Place in a pot and heat.

For either dried or canned beans, place the olive oil in a small pot and heat until it is hot enough to sizzle when a sage leaf is dropped into it. Add the sage leaves and turn them over. It will take only a minute until they are done. Remove from the heat and let cool a little. Place the beans in a serving bowl and pour the olive oil and sage leaves over them. Add the sea salt and pepper at this time.

Chickpea Patties - Garbanzo Patties

*Polpettine di ceci*

2/3 cup dry garbanzo (ceci) beans or 1 15 oz. can of garbanzo (ceci) beans (either equals about 1 2/3 cups cooked beans)

1 egg beaten

1 small to medium onion peeled and chopped into a small dice

3 stalks celery

¼ cup finely chopped parsley

¼ cup whole wheat flour

extra virgin olive oil (enough to cover your sauté pan by ¼ inch)

For the dried beans:

Follow the directions for soaking and cooking the beans on page 101.

For canned beans:

Drain the beans and rinse them under cold water.

Cut off the bottom of the celery and cut off the tips of the celery stalks by about ¼ of an inch, if the ends are dried out. Thoroughly rinse off the celery to remove any dirt. Remove any tough strings from the stalks by placing your knife under the strings and pulling them lengthwise down the celery stalk, or remove the strings with a vegetable peeler by shaving a thin layer off. Cut the celery into a small dice.

Drain the cooked beans or drain and rinse the cans of beans and place in a large bowl. Mash them quite thoroughly. A potato masher works well for this. Add the beaten egg, the chopped onion, the chopped celery, the chopped parsley, and the whole wheat flour. Mix together thoroughly, either with a large spoon or your hands which will work best. Form into small patties about 1 ½ inches in diameter.

Heat the olive oil over medium high heat until it sizzles when a small piece of ceci mixture is dropped into it. Gently place the patties into your sauté pan and sauté them until they are a golden brown on the bottom about 3 minutes, turn them over with a metal spatula and scrape up any browned bits. Sauté the patties on the other side until they are a beautiful golden brown on both sides. Remove the patties from the pan, and place them on a plate lined with paper toweling to drain them. Place on a serving platter and serve, or place them on an oven-proof serving platter and place the platter in a warm oven until you are ready to serve them.

## Roasted Chickpeas

## Ceci arrosta

2/3 cup dry beans or 1 can 15 oz. canned beans (either equals about 1 2/3 cups cooked beans)

extra virgin olive oil for coating a baking sheet

salt to taste

For the dried beans:

Follow the directions for soaking and cooking the beans on page 101.

For canned beans:

Drain the beans and rinse them under cold water.

Coat a rimmed baking sheet with olive oil. Spread the ceci beans on the baking sheet and place in a preheated 350 degree Fahrenheit oven. Roast until they are slightly crisp on the outside and tender on the inside. Sprinkle with salt and serve.

# Miscellaneous

## *Aggegi vari*

## How to Supreme an Orange or Grapefruit

*Arancia*

Removing the citrus sections from the membranes makes the fruit especially tender and juicy.

Peel the fruit, going deep enough to cut off all of the white membrane (the pith). Once the fruit is peeled, hold the fruit in one hand over a bowl to catch all the juices, and with your other hand slice with a sharp paring knife right alongside of the membrane down to the center core. Slice on the other side of the section on the inside of the membrane down to the core. Try to stay as close to the membrane as you can to remove as much of each section as possible. Remove the skinless section and repeat until all of the sections have been removed.

Squeeze the remaining membrane into the bowl with the juice, to extract as much orange juice as possible. The juice can be squeezed over the sections or used for something else.

## Sautéed Garlic

### Aglio saltati

This is very useful to have in your refrigerator, it can be added to pasta dishes to give them a flavor boost, and is a delicious addition to vinaigrettes.

1 head of garlic peeled and finely chopped

2 tablespoons butter

Heat the butter in a small sauté pan over medium heat. Place the finely chopped garlic into the butter once it is hot enough to sizzle when a piece of garlic is dropped into the butter. Watch the garlic very closely to make sure that it does not burn. It should only turn golden. Lower the heat and sauté, stirring occasionally and watching it carefully so that it does not overly darken. Sauté until the garlic is fragrant and golden on all sides.

Sautéed Leeks

*Porri saltati*

3 medium size leeks

3 Tbsp. butter

sea salt to taste

freshly ground pepper to taste (optional)

Cut off the root ends and the dark green tops of the leeks. Slice in half lengthwise and rinse under cold running water to remove any sand or dirt. Cut into a small dice of about 1/3 to ½ inch.

Heat the butter in a medium size sauté pan or skillet. Add the chopped leeks when the butter is hot enough to sizzle when a piece of leek is dropped into it. Sauté the leeks in the butter over medium heat, for 5 minutes or so, stirring occasionally. Watch them carefully to make sure that they do not burn. Sauté until the leeks are soft and translucent.

## Breadcrumbs

*Pangrattato*

### Fresh Breadcrumbs

Crusts are optional you may remove them or leave them on. Tear each slice of bread into 4 or 5 pieces and place in a food processor, and pulse on and off until the breadcrumbs are the size you desire.

1 slice of fresh bread equals about 1 cup of breadcrumbs.

### Crumbled Fresh Breadcrumbs

Remove the crusts and crumble the bread slice between your fingers. This method is quick and if you do not have a food processor at your disposal or you want to quickly have breadcrumbs this is a good method. The crumbs will be a little larger.

### Dried Breadcrumbs

You may remove the crusts or leave them on. Place the bread slices on a cookie sheet and place in a preheated 250 degree Fahrenheit oven for 5 to 7 minutes, then turn over the slices and dry out for another 5 to 7 minutes. The bread should be dry and crisp, lightly golden is fine but do not let the slices turn brown. Place in a food processor and pulse until you have reached the desired size of breadcrumbs. If you wish you can grate the bread on a box grater or place the dried slices of bread between two sheets of waxed paper and crush the bread into crumbs with a rolling pin. The bread must be very dry for the last two methods.

1 slice of dried bread equals about ¼ cup of breadcrumbs.

Skillet Dried Breadcrumbs

Place the breadcrumbs in a dry skillet and place over medium heat. Stir them as they start to turn golden. Keep stirring until they reach a beautiful golden brown.

Breadcrumbs with Olive Oil

2 Tbsp. extra virgin olive oil

1 cup dried breadcrumbs

Salt and freshly ground pepper to taste (optional)

These breadcrumbs are delicious with just the olive oil, but if you are topping a mild dish that needs more salt and pepper, add them to taste.

Heat the olive oil in a skillet over medium heat and when the oil is hot add the breadcrumbs and toss to coat.  If you are using the salt and pepper add them at this time. Toss once again and remove from the heat.

Buttered Breadcrumbs

2 Tbsp. butter

1 cup dried breadcrumbs

Salt and pepper to taste (optional)

These breadcrumbs are delicious with just the butter, but if you are topping a mild dish, or you want more seasonings, add the salt and pepper to taste. Heat the butter over medium heat and when the butter is hot add the breadcrumbs and toss to coat. If you are using the salt and pepper add them at this time. Toss once again and remove from the heat.

Lemon and Parsley Breadcrumbs

2 Tbsp. extra virgin olive oil

1 cup dried breadcrumbs

1 tsp. finely chopped garlic

1 Tbsp. finely grated lemon zest

2 Tbsp. finely chopped parsley

coarse sea salt to taste

freshly ground pepper to taste

Heat the olive oil in a skillet and add the garlic, when the oil is hot enough that it begins to sizzle when a piece of chopped garlic is dropped into it. Sauté the garlic stirring frequently until the garlic is golden. Add the lemon zest and cook another 30 seconds to a minute, until it is fragrant. Add the parsley, and then the breadcrumbs. Toss everything together and remove from the heat.

Herbed Breadcrumbs

2 Tbsp. extra virgin olive oil

1 cup dried breadcrumbs

1 tsp. finely chopped garlic

2 tsp. finely chopped fresh rosemary

2 Tbsp. finely chopped fresh parsley

2 tsp. dried oregano

Heat the olive oil in a skillet and add the garlic, when the oil is hot enough that it begins to sizzle when a piece of chopped garlic is dropped into it. Sauté the garlic stirring frequently until the garlic is golden. Add the rosemary, parsley, and the oregano, stir and then add the breadcrumbs. Mix everything together and remove from the heat.

## Mayonnaise

*Maionese*

2 egg yolks at room temperature

1 to 1 1/3 cup extra virgin olive oil at room temperature

1 to 2 Tbsp. freshly squeezed lemon juice at room temperature

salt to taste

The ingredients must be at room temperature to help prevent the mayonnaise from separating. Place the yolks in a bowl and beat them with a hand held mixer, or a balloon wire whisk. Beat the egg yolks until they are a very pale yellow and creamy.

Start to add the olive oil a drop at a time while beating constantly. Stop pouring the oil every few seconds (while continuing to beat the yolks) to check to make sure that the oil is thoroughly mixed in. Continue beating and adding oil until the mayonnaise is quite thick. Add ½ tsp. of the lemon juice and continue beating. The sauce will become a little thinner at this point. Start dribbling the oil in a little faster while you continue to beat. Check frequently to make sure that the yolks are completely absorbing the oil. Add more lemon juice as needed to keep the sauce from getting to thick. When 1 cup of the oil is completely emulsified you may stop adding oil. If you think that the sauce needs more oil, and you are confidant that the sauce will take more oil, proceed cautiously and very slowly to add some or all of the remaining oil. When you have added all the oil that you are going to add , mix the salt to taste and the rest of the lemon juice to taste in a small bowl (this helps the salt to dissolve,) and slowly add the lemon juice and salt mixture while beating constantly. Place in the refrigerator if you are not using it immediately.

## Aïoli

This is my version of aioli. In the traditional preparation you start with raw garlic, and grind it in a mortal and pestle, then add olive oil very slowly. I prefer to have the garlic cooked.

1 cup Mayonnaise page 115 or good quality commercial mayonnaise

8 cloves of Roasted Garlic page 88 at room temperature

Remove the garlic (it should be soft) from the roasted head of garlic and mash the garlic with a fork, add a tablespoon of mayonnaise and thoroughly mash together with your fork. Add the rest of the mayonnaise and combine thoroughly. Refrigerate until you are ready to serve the aïoli.

## Sour Cream and Onion Dip

This is my homemade version of onion dip. There are no additives which in my opinion is always a plus. It is delicious, and gets better if allowed to sit in the refrigerator for at least an hour before serving.

1 cup sour cream

1 tsp. onion powder

Mix the onion powder into the sour cream thoroughly and refrigerate until you are ready to serve it.

## Light Dip

This has a very light feel to it, and takes only a minute or so to make.

½ cup sour cream

½ cup Mayonnaise  page 115 or purchased mayonnaise

Mix together thoroughly and serve or refrigerate.

This is very good with raw vegetables.

Béchamel

*Balsamella*

2 Tbsp. butter

2 Tbsp. all-purpose unbleached flour

1/8 tsp. salt

1/8 tsp. pepper

¾ cup whole milk or half and half, or cream

½ cup chicken stock (Browned Chicken Stock page 30 or good quality purchased chicken stock

Melt the butter in a heavy bottomed saucepan over low heat. When the butter is completely melted and bubbling, add the flour, salt and pepper. Use a wooden spoon to stir while cooking over low heat. When the mixture is smooth and bubbly remove it from the heat and add the cream. Return to the heat and stir to mix thoroughly, then add the chicken stock and return to a boil while stirring constantly. Boil for one minute and remove from the heat.

Toasted Walnuts

*Noci arrosta*

Keeping the heat low preserves the nutritious value of the nuts

20 to 25 walnut halves

extra virgin olive oil just enough to coat the nuts

Place the walnuts on a baking sheet and add enough olive oil to coat the walnuts very lightly. Place them in a preheated 175 degrees Fahrenheit oven. Roast for 4 to 5 minutes.

Toasted Pine Nuts

*Pinoli arrosta*

Watch these very closely as you toast them, they burn easily.

3 oz. pine nuts (from Italy preferably)

Place the pine nuts on a rimmed baking sheet and place in a preheated 350 degree Fahrenheit oven for about 10 minutes. After 5 minutes stir them and let toast for another 3 to 5 minutes until they are golden. Remove from the oven and remove them from the baking sheet to stop them from burning.

Alternatively you can toast them in a dry skillet. Stir them as they toast. When they are a golden brown remove them from the heat and remove them from the pan so as not to let them burn.

Baked Potatoes

*Patate al forno*

4 russet potatoes

soft butter

sour cream

finely chopped chives (optional)

sea salt and freshly ground black pepper

Rinse the potatoes under cold water to remove any dirt. Place on a flat surface and make a slit lengthwise down the middle of the potato.

Place on the middle rack of your oven that has been preheated to 350 degrees Fahrenheit. Bake 45 minutes to 1 hour until the center of the potatoes are soft all the way through.

Serve with butter and sour cream and the optional chopped chives for your guests to add to their individual potatoes.

Completely peeling the potatoes before you make a slit in them makes a delicious variation on baked potatoes. The potatoes form a shell that is crispy and completely edible.

# Entrees

## *Secondi Piatti*

## Standing Rib Roast with Roasted Potatoes

*Arrosto con patate*

This beautiful dinner is what my Mother often prepared for our family's Sunday mid-day meal. In Italian families The Sunday noon meal is traditionally the largest and most celebratory meal of the week. While I usually do not make a large dinner for the Sunday noon meal, this is a dish that I love and serve often. This makes a splendid dinner for a holiday or any special occasion or a special dinner for special guests and especially as a wonderful dinner for the family.

short end rib roast (3 ribs makes an excellent roast)about 5 lbs. *

kosher salt and freshly ground black pepper

8 medium sized russet potatoes

1 to 2 Tbsp. butter if needed

Trim off excess fat, leaving enough fat for the meat and potatoes to roast in. Season the roast with salt and pepper on all sides. Place rib side down in a pan that has sides no higher than 2 inches, (you do not want the meat to steam) and is large enough to hold the roast and the potatoes that will be added later very comfortably. Place in a preheated 350 degree Fahrenheit oven. Roast for about 1 1/2 hours at 350 degrees, then turn the heat up to 400 degrees Fahrenheit a few minutes before adding the potatoes. The potatoes should be peeled and cut into 1 to 2inch chunks. Dry the potatoes completely with paper toweling then place them around the roast in the roasting pan. Roast for approximately 45 minutes. As the potatoes brown and get crispy on the outside, turn them until they are browned and crispy on all sides and tender on the inside. If the potatoes need more fat, about 1 to 2 tablespoons of butter can be added as they brown.

*Roasting time should be 30 to 35 minutes per lb. of roast. Medium rare is an internal temperature of 145 degrees Fahrenheit. Medium is an internal temperature of 160 degrees Fahrenheit. Well done is an internal temperature of 170 degrees Fahrenheit.

Remove the roast from the oven and place it on a large platter. Let the roast rest for a few minutes. Remove the potatoes from the oven scraping up any potato bits that have stuck to the roasting pan. Place potatoes and potato bits around the roast.

Serve and enjoy. Serves 8

Asparagus with Olive Oil (page 73), Brussels Sprouts Roasted in Olive Oil (page 78), Simple Brussels Sprouts (page 80), and Sautéed Spinach (page 72), all complement the roast and potatoes very well. Roasted garlic (page 88) is very nice with the roast and potatoes also.

Beef Tenderloin with Crispy Potato Cakes

*Filetto con patate*

4 medallions of beef tenderloin (each about 1 to 1 ½ inches thick)

4 tsp. butter (1 tsp. butter for each medallion of tenderloin)

4 medium russet potatoes

butter for sautéing the potato cakes

kosher salt and freshly ground pepper to taste

Season the tenderloin medallions with kosher salt and freshly ground pepper. Place 1 tsp. of butter under each medallion in an oven proof skillet or sauté pan. Place in a preheated 350 degree Fahrenheit oven. Roast until the fillet is brown and caramelized on the outside and the desired doneness is reached on the inside. Allow the medallions to rest for 5 minutes before serving.

While the medallions are roasting peel the potatoes and cut into chunks. Place the chunks in a food processor and use the shredding disc to shred the potatoes. If you do not have a food processor you can use the largest holes of a box grater. Form the potatoes into 4 potato cakes. Heat enough butter to coat the bottom of a sauté pan or skillet generously and when it is hot enough to sizzle when a piece of shredded potato is dropped into it, add the potato cakes. Sauté the potato cakes until they are golden brown on one side, then turn them over with a metal spatula scraping up any browned bits, and sauté until they are golden brown on the other side and cooked through.

Place the potato cakes on individual plates and place a tenderloin medallion alongside of each cake.

Serve Aïoli (page 116) along with the potatoes and medallions.

Beef Tenderloin with Mushrooms

*Filetto con funghi*

Use the center cut of the tenderloin if you can. This is the most tender and delicious part of the tenderloin. I suggest that you keep the side dishes rather simple as the dish is so flavorful it should be the centerpiece of the meal.

1 to 1 ½ lb. beef tenderloin

kosher salt and freshl y ground pepper

7 to 8 cloves of garlic peeled and finely chopped

2 packages (8 oz. each) button mushrooms (peeled-optional instructions for peeling on page 46) rinsed and the ends of the stems removed if they are dry looking

Trim any silver skin (the sinewy skin) off the tenderloin. Generously salt and pepper the loin on all sides at this time also.

Place in a preheated 350 degree Fahrenheit oven. Roast until desired doneness is reached. For medium-well about 30 to 35 minutes.

While the meat is roasting heat the butter in a small sauté pan and when the butter is hot enough to sizzle when a piece of garlic is dropped into it add the garlic. Sauté until the garlic is a very light golden color. Remove from the heat and set aside. The garlic will finish in the oven with the roast.

Cut the mushrooms into quarters and place in a medium size saucepan. The liquid in the mushrooms will give off enough moisture to cook them. Place over medium heat and stir them occasionally as they cook. Watch them to make sure that they do not burn. When they are cooked through and their liquid has reduced a little remove from the heat.

About 10 minutes before the tenderloin reaches your desired doneness place the garlic and butter mixture around the roast. After another 5 minutes pour the mushrooms and their juice over the meat. Leave the roast in the oven until it reaches the doneness that you prefer.

Baked Potatoes (page122) go very well with this, as well as Brussels Sprouts Roasted in Olive Oil (page 78) or Simple Brussels Sprouts (page 80)

Lamb Stew

*Stufatino di agnello*

This is a very comforting dish and is especially good on a cold day.

2 to 3 Tbsp. butter

3 ½ lbs. boneless leg of lamb

5 cloves garlic peeled and finely chopped

1 can 1 lb. 12 oz. (28 oz.) peeled tomatoes, preferably organic

5 carrots peeled and cut into 1/3 inch slices

½ of a 9 oz. pkg. baby green peas

5 medium potatoes peeled and cut into large chunks

Salt and freshly ground pepper

Cut the lamb into 1 inch chunks or cubes and season with salt and pepper. Place the butter in a large heavy bottomed pot and when it is hot enough to sizzle when a piece of lamb is dropped into it, add the lamb chunks. Brown the lamb on all sides. When they are almost caramelized on all sides, add the chopped garlic. When the garlic is a light golden color, and the meat is golden brown and caramelized on all sides add the tomatoes and their juice. Turn the heat up to medium high and bring to a simmer, stirring occasionally. Once it is bubbling turn the heat down to low, cover and simmer very gently for 30 to 40 minutes. Add the sliced carrots and baby peas. Cover and simmer another 30 minutes until done. Meanwhile during the last 20 minutes of cooking time, boil the potatoes in salted water. Add the potatoes at the very end. You may add a little of the potato cooking water if the sauce has become too thick. If you use the potato cooking water, be sure it is very hot when you are adding it so that it does not toughen the meat.

Serve piping hot.

Italian bread (page 20), or Toasted Garlic Bread (page 7) go so well with this dish. A salad with vinaigrette such as Green Salad (page 164) also goes nicely with this. A vegetable such as Green Beans with Butter (page 71) is a favorite of mine to serve with this.

## Lamb Chops Sautéed with Garlic

*Costolette di agnello saltate all'aglio*

This is wonderful and very simple while at the same time very elegant. This is a dish that I make very frequently, and I love the beautiful aroma that fills up the house when you make these. My mother Marguerite who is 98 was still preparing this dish at 95 and it is still one of her favorites. Served with a few sides (some are listed at the end of this recipe that I think go well with these lamb chops) will give you a beautiful meal that should put smiles on the faces of your family and guests.

6 thin rib lamb chops

4 or 5 garlic cloves peeled and finely chopped

1 Tbsp. butter

kosher salt and freshly ground pepper to taste

Trim the fat off of the lamb chops and take the silver skin off of the outside of the meat. Season both sides of the lamb chops with salt and pepper. Melt the butter in a large skillet or sauté pan that is oven proof over medium high heat. Gently add the lamb chops to the butter when it has reached the point that it sizzles when a lamb chop is added to it. Sauté the lamb chops in the butter until they are nicely browned on one side. Turn over the chops and add the finely chopped garlic. Brown the chops on the other side, and scrape up the little brown bits on the bottom of the pan into the butter. Watch carefully to make sure that nothing burns. Transfer the pan to a preheated 350 degree Fahrenheit oven. Leave in the oven 10 to 15 minutes until they reach the doneness that you prefer. Remove from the oven and place on a warmed platter and serve as soon as possible.

A simple vegetable side dish of Asparagus with Olive Oil (page 73) (if they are in season) goes very well with this dish. Broccoli with Olive Oil (page 70) or

Brussels Sprouts Roasted in Olive Oil (page 78) also makes a nice side for this. Served with a salad that is dressed with a vinaigrette such as Green Salad (page 164), and a potato dish such as Mashed Potatoes with Leeks Sautéed in Olive Oil (page 97), or Potato Gratin (page 95), or simply a Baked Potato (page 122).

Leg of Lamb with Roasted Potatoes

*Agnello al forno con papate*

This makes a beautiful celebratory meal. It is a dish that is easy to prepare and is delicious and makes a great presentation.

Bone-in leg of lamb (about 3 ½ to 4 lbs.)

4 cloves of garlic peeled and cut into fourths lengthwise

kosher salt and freshly ground black pepper

8 medium size russet potatoes

butter

Remove the silver skin (the sinewy skin) and any excess fat, leaving enough fat on the lamb to melt and be used for the potatoes to roast in. Cut slits about 2 inches apart into the leg of lamb and push a piece of garlic into each slit. Season the meat with salt and pepper on all sides. Place in a pan that has sides no higher than 2 inches, (you do not want the meat to steam,) and is large enough to comfortably hold the leg of lamb and the potatoes that will be added later.

Place in a preheated 350 degree Fahrenheit oven. Roast 45 to 60 minutes at 350 degrees.

Turn the heat up to 400 degrees Fahrenheit for a few minutes before adding the potatoes. The potatoes should be peeled and cut into 1 to 1 1/2inch chunks. Dry the potatoes completely with paper toweling, then add them to the roasting pan. As the potatoes brown and get crispy on the outside, turn them scraping up the browned potatoes with a large metal spoon. Roast until they are browned and crispy on all sides and tender on the inside about 30 minutes to an hour depending on the size of the chunks of potato. If the potatoes need more fat, add 1 to 2 tablespoons of butter as they brown. When the lamb has reached the desired doneness, 175 to 180 degrees Fahrenheit internal temperature remove the lamb from the oven and place it on a large platter. Let the lamb rest a few minutes. Remove the potatoes from the oven scraping up any potato bits that have stuck to the roasting pan. Place potatoes and potato bits around the lamb.

Roasting time should be approximately 25 to 30 minutes per lb. depending on desired doneness

Serve and enjoy.

Carrots Roasted with Olive Oil (page 77) goes well with leg of lamb as does Sautéed Spinach (page 72) as well as Buttered Leeks (page 87).

Serves 6

Chicken with Plum Tomatoes and Fusilli

*Pollo con pomadori*

7 or 8 boneless and skinless chicken breasts

3 Tbsp. extra virgin olive oil

2 Tbsp. butter

1 medium sized onion

5 cloves of garlic

kosher salt and freshly ground black pepper

10 or 11 fresh plum tomatoes or 2 cans of 18 oz. plum tomatoes San Marzano if they are available to you

¼ cup chopped parsley

1 box 16 oz. box of fusilli or if you prefer a 16 oz. box of penne rigate pasta

Parmigiano-Reggiano or Grana Padano for grating

Rinse and dry the chicken breasts. Season the breasts with the salt and pepper. Heat the butter and olive oil together in a large skillet or sauté pan. Meanwhile peel and very finely mince the garlic, and chop the onion into a small dice.

Add the finely minced garlic into your sauté pan or skillet when the butter and olive oil has been heated to the point that it sizzles when a piece of garlic is dropped into it. Sauté for a couple of minutes and when the garlic is softening and very light add the chopped onion. Stir with a wooden spoon, being very careful not to burn the garlic. When the onion is totally translucent, add the chicken breasts. Sauté the chicken breasts until they are a nice golden brown on one side, then turn them over and sauté on the other side until they are a nice golden brown on both sides.

While the chicken breasts are sautéing, prepare the tomatoes. If you are using fresh tomatoes they should be peeled. Use one of the following three methods. The third method is quick and works well with fully ripe tomatoes.

Peeling Tomatoes:

1. Slow-roast and peel (place the tomatoes in a pre-heated 350 degree Fahrenheit oven for 3 to 5 minutes or when the skins are starting to crack, then remove them from the oven.)

2. Blanch the tomatoes in boiling water 1 or 2 at a time. Let them sit in the boiling water for a minute or two and then remove then them from the boiling water.

With either of the above methods, you need to let them cool before peeling them. Either place in a bowl of ice water to cool them quickly or let them sit out until they are cool enough to handle.

3. Peel the tomatoes with a paring knife or a plastic serrated tomato knife, or other serrated plastic knife such as a disposable plastic flatware knife.

Now place the fresh tomatoes or the canned tomatoes in a large bowl and break them up with your hands or a potato masher. When the chicken breasts are a nice golden brown on all sides, add the tomatoes. Cover and simmer for 20 minutes.

While the chicken is simmering, prepare the fusilli or penne. Place a large pot of water on to boil. When it reaches a boil add the kosher salt and the pasta, return to a boil, and cook according to the package directions.

Add the chopped parsley to the sauce and simmer uncovered for another 5 minutes. When the pasta is almost al dente,(tender but firm to the bite) add it to the chicken and sauce and let it finish cooking in the sauce. Taste for seasoning and adjust if necessary. The pasta should be al dente and the chicken should be done and very tender. Place in a large ovenproof bowl that has been warmed in a 150 degree Fahrenheit oven.

Serve with freshly grated Parmigiano-Reggiano or Grana Padano, alongside for each person to sprinkle on his or her serving.

A slice of Italian Bread (page 20) or Toasted Garlic Bread (page 7), goes well with this, as well as a salad with a vinegar and olive oil dressing such as Green Salad (page 164)

Chicken with Tomato Sauce and Fusilli

*Pollo al potacchio*

Potacchio is the sauce that is added to the chicken to finish cooking it.

1 3 to 3 ½ pound chicken (preferably organic) cut into pieces

3 Tbsp. extra virgin olive oil

2 Tbsp. butter

16 oz. box of fusilli pasta

Parmigiano-Reggiano or Grana Padano for grating

Potacchio Sauce

1 medium sized onion

extra virgin olive oil (enough to coat the bottom of your pot)

3 cloves garlic

1 sprig of fresh rosemary

¼ cup chopped parsley

8 or 9 fresh tomatoes or 1 can 18 0z. of peeled plum tomatoes or 1 can of tomato puree 29 oz. (1 lb 13 oz.)

If you are using fresh tomatoes they should be peeled. Use one of the three methods on page 136.

Place the fresh tomatoes or the canned tomatoes in a large bowl and break them up with your hands or a potato masher, or coarsely chop with a knife. Peel and finely mince the garlic. Peel and chop the onion into a medium size dice.

Heat the olive in a large pot. Place the finely minced garlic into the olive oil once it has reached the point that it sizzles when a piece of garlic is added to it. Sauté and stir with a wooden spoon, being very careful not to let the garlic burn. When the garlic is starting to turn a very light golden color add the chopped onion. When the onion is totally translucent, add the chopped tomato or the tomato puree. Add the salt and pepper to taste. Add the rosemary and simmer for 20 to 30 minutes.

Rinse and dry the chicken pieces. Season the chicken pieces with salt and freshly ground pepper. Gently add the chicken pieces into your sauté pan or skillet with the butter and olive oil that has been heated to the point that it sizzles when a piece of chicken is added to it. Sauté the chicken pieces until they are a nice golden brown on one side, then turn them over and sauté on the other side until they are a nice golden brown on both sides. Add the Potacchio and cover. Simmer for another 25 to 30 min. While the chicken is simmering, prepare the fusilli. Place a large pot of water on to boil. When it reaches a boil add the kosher salt and the pasta, return to a boil, and cook according to the package directions. Once the fussili is almost al dente (tender but firm to the bite), add it to the potacchino and chicken. Simmer uncovered for another 5 minutes and add the chopped parsley and simmer another 5 minutes. Taste for seasoning and adjust if necessary. The pasta should be al dente, and the chicken should be done and very tender. Place in a large ovenproof bowl that has been warmed in a 150 degree Fahrenheit oven. Serve some freshly grated Parmigiano-Reggiano or Grana Padano, alongside for each person to sprinkle on his or her serving.

Toasted Garlic Bread (page 7) goes well with this. A salad with vinegar and olive oil dressing such as Mixed Salad) (page 166) is also very nice with this dish.

Apricot Glazed Chicken Breasts or Orange Glazed Chicken Breasts

*Petti di pollo*

The apricot glazed chicken breasts or the orange marmalade glazed chicken breasts are so easy, and so spectacular. These dishes can be prepared on a busy day without much fuss. They make a great main course on a busy day or when you are having guests. They are so good and they do not take much time to prepare, leaving you time for other things including of course your guests.

4 chicken breasts bone-in and skins on

kosher salt and freshly ground pepper

1 jar (12 oz.) apricot preserves for apricot glaze or

1 jar (12 oz.) orange marmalade for orange glaze

Season the chicken breasts with the salt and pepper on all sides, and put them in an oven proof dish skin side up. Place into a preheated 350 degree Fahrenheit oven and roast until lightly browned about 1 hour. At this point about 20 minutes before the chicken is done remove the roasting pan with the chicken breasts from the oven and spoon the apricot preserves or the orange marmalade over the chicken breasts until they are all well covered. Place them back into the oven and continue roasting until the chicken is cooked through and is golden brown, and the sauce is bubbling and starting to caramelize. You will need to watch carefully at this point so as not to burn the sauce. Remove from the oven and transfer to a serving platter. Spoon off the fat in the roasting pan and place the remaining sauce into a serving bowl to serve at the table.

You can substitute boneless and skinless chicken breasts. This will reduce the calories but unfortunately will also reduce the flavor. I suggest that you try them both ways, both with the bone-in and skin on, and boneless and skinless. If you use boneless and skinless breasts you will need to reduce the roasting time before you add the apricot preserves or orange marmalade  by about half (25 to 30 minutes).

Gratin of Celery with Béchamel (page 86) goes well with these as well as Celery Fried in Olive Oil  (page 83) and Buttered Leeks (page 87), a Baked Potato (page 122) or Mashed Potatoes with Leeks Sautéed in Olive Oil Leeks (page 97) and a salad with a vinaigrette such as Green Salad (page 164).

Chicken Breasts in Sherry

4 boneless and skinless chicken breasts

unbleached all-purpose flour for dredging

salt and freshly ground pepper

2 Tbsp. butter

1 Tbsp. extra virgin olive oil

¾ cup dry sherry or Marsala divided

1 head garlic peeled and finely chopped

1 to 2 Tbsp. extra virgin olive oil for sautéing garlic

2 packages (8 oz. each) white button mushrooms rinsed and (peeled - optional instructions for peeling on page 46) and cut into quarters

1 Tbsp. butter to finish the dish at the end (optional)

2 Tbsp. chopped parsley (optional)

1 lb. package (16 oz.) fusilli

kosher salt for the pasta cooking water

Remove any sinews from the chicken breasts and flatten with a meat mallet or if you do not have a meat mallet you can take a small skillet or sauté pan to flatten the breasts. Season the flour with the salt and pepper. Dredge the breasts in the flour mixture and shake off the excess. Gently add the chicken pieces into a sauté pan or skillet with the 2 Tbsp. butter and 1 Tbsp. olive oil that has been heated to the point that it sizzles when a piece of chicken is added to it. Sauté until the breasts are a light golden color on one side, then turn over and sauté until the breasts are a golden color on both sides. Add ½ cup of the sherry or Marsala and cook through (about 15 minutes). The chicken should continue to brown.

While the chicken is cooking, sauté the garlic in 1 to 2 Tbsp extra virgin olive oil.

Also while the chicken is cooking, place the quartered mushrooms in a small pot and cook them over medium heat. There is enough moisture in the mushrooms to cook them without adding anything else.

Place a large pot of water on to boil. When it reaches a boil add the kosher salt and the pasta, return to a boil, and cook according to the package directions.

When the chicken is cooked through and the pasta is almost al-dente (tender but firm to the bite), add it to the chicken using a metal spider or a large slotted metal spoon. Reserve a small amount of the pasta water. Add the sautéed garlic and the cooked mushrooms to the chicken breasts. Turn up the heat and add the remaining ¼ cup Marsala. Season to taste with salt and pepper. Add the optional Tbsp. of butter if desired and add a little pasta water if necessary. If you are using the optional parsley add it now. Serve and enjoy.

## Roast Chicken

*Pollo arrosto al forno*

This is simplicity itself, and it is in my opinion the best way to roast a chicken. I have heard that one way to distinguish a talented cook is by their roast chicken. This method has worked for generations in my family. I hope you will enjoy it also. It is wonderful.

1 chicken about 2 ½ to 3 lbs.

kosher salt

freshly ground pepper (optional)

Rinse the chicken inside and out under cold running water. Remove any stray pieces from inside of the chicken. If any neck has been left on, trim that off. Trim the tail end off also if that has been left on. Place the chicken on a rack that has been placed over a roasting pan or other pan big enough to catch all the dripping from the chicken. Use a generous amount of kosher salt to salt the inside of the bird and all over the outside of the bird. If you are using the freshly ground pepper sprinkle it judiciously on the inside and outside.

Place in a preheated 350 degree Fahrenheit oven, and let it roast for about 2 hours. It is done when you can very easily break off a drumstick.

Turkey Stuffed with Black Olives

*Tacchino con olive nere*

This is a very simple way to roast a turkey and as far as I am concerned the very best way. This is the method my mother, Marguerite and my grandmother Rosalie used to prepare a holiday bird. This roasting method was always used on Thanksgiving, and if a turkey was served on Christmas, or Easter this method was used as well. The flavor of the olives becomes rich and full. As a child I would always be in the kitchen as the turkey was taken out of the oven so that I could have a few of the olives out of the cavity, before the presentation of the grand bird.

1 medium sized turkey 8 to 10 pounds fresh and organic if available (if you are serving a large crowd prepare 2 turkeys, rather than one large bird as the meat tends to dry out and be tougher than the younger and more tender smaller birds.)

15 or more olives (regular black olives are fine, but you can use any variety of black olive that you prefer)

kosher salt and freshly ground black pepper

large shallow roasting pan (you want to have the bird exposed to the air, so that it does not steam)

rack to place the turkey on (an ovenproof cookie cooling rack works well)

Remove giblets and liver if they are stored in the cavity. Rinse your turkey under cold running water, and remove any veins or membranes that are in the cavity of the bird, as well as you can. Place the bird on a rack inside of, or sitting on top of a roasting pan. The rack should keep the bird at least ½ inch of the bottom of the pan. Use a roasting pan with plenty of room to hold the bird comfortably. The roasting pan should have sides about 2 inches high, this will be high enough to make gravy after the bird is roasted and low enough to have air circulate around the bird adequately to ensure even cooking of both the white and dark meat. Generously salt the inside of the cavity, lift the bird and place it breast side down on the rack and salt and pepper the back of the bird. Lift the bird once again and place it on it's back and proceed to salt and pepper the breast and legs and wings. Place in a 350 degree Fahrenheit oven for the appropriate amount of time for the weight of the bird. Approximately 1 ½ to 2 hours for every 5 pounds. When you are about 45 minutes away from the bird being done, place the olives in the cavity of the bird. When the bird is done, you should be able to remove the drumstick without much resistance. The bird should have reached an internal temperature of 180 degrees Fahrenheit. If you are using a meat thermometer insert the thermometer into the breast without touching the bone. Remove the bird from the oven and let it rest. Remove all of the olives from the cavity and reserve 5 or so for garnish. Place the rest in a serving dish and keep warm. Place the bird on a warm platter. Place orange slices and olives around the turkey decoratively. You are now ready to enjoy a bird that is fit for a King or Queen. Buon Appetito!

Calves Liver with Butter

*Fegato con cipolla*

My mother, Marguerite made this dish as a lunch for herself and me, when I was a child. I used to call the pan that she cooked the liver in, the million dollar pan. I loved to scrape up any bits from the pan and eat it with a piece of crusty bread. It is so good!

½ Lb. calves liver (organic if possible)

2 Tbsp. butter

A pinch of salt and a pinch of freshly ground black pepper

several slices of a good quality, crusty Italian or French bread

Remove any outer skin (membrane) from the outer edges of the liver. Sometimes it pulls off quite easily, but sometimes you have to slice it off. Also remove any membranes from the interior of the liver around any holes (tubes). Cut the liver into pieces of about 1 inch by 2 inches. Heat the butter over medium high heat in a sauté pan large enough to easily accommodate all of the liver. Add the liver when the butter has been heated to the point that it sizzles when a piece of liver is added to it. Turn over the liver pieces when they are brown and caramelized on the bottom side and cook until the liver is brown and caramelized on the other side, about 4 to 5 minutes on each side. If the pan starts to become dry, add another teaspoon of butter as needed. You may have to add more than one before the liver is done. When the liver is a beautiful brown and cooked all the way through, remove the pan from the heat. Remove the liver and scrape up any frond (tasty bits) from the bottom of the pan, and spread it on a slice of the crusty bread. Serve immediately, you will have the easiest and tastiest liver imaginable.

Veal Chops with Tomatoes and Fusilli Pasta

*Nodini di vitellocon pomodori*

This is a dish my mother Marguerite would make very often. It filled our house with a rich wonderful aroma. There are not many ingredients in this dish, but it has a mellow rich flavor that is unsurpassed.

4 loin veal chops

1 Tbsp. butter

4 or 5 fresh tomatoes peeled and coarsely chopped (directions for peeling fresh tomatoes on page 136), or 1 can (1 lb. 12 oz.) peeled plum tomatoes coarsely chopped

salt and white pepper to taste

1 lb. package (16 oz.) of fussillli pasta

1 Tbsp kosher salt for the pasta water

Trim the skin and most of the fat from the outside edges of the veal chops. Place the chops between 2 sheets of plastic wrap and pound with a mallet, or a small heavy skillet a few times to ensure chops will be tender. Do not over pound, you want to tenderize the veal chops not to flatten them. The chops should remain almost ½ inch thick. Season to taste with salt and white pepper.

Melt the butter in a large skillet or sauté pan, over medium high heat. Gently add the veal chops to the butter when it has reached the point that it sizzles when a veal chop is added to it. Let the chops lightly brown on one side before turning them over. The chops should turn a nice golden brown on the second side. At this point, it is time to add the coarsely chopped tomatoes and the juices from the tomatoes. Stir the tomatoes around in the butter and make sure the chops are not sticking to the bottom of the pan. Turn the heat down to a low simmer and cover the pan. Simmer the tomatoes and chops for around 25 minutes. While the chops are simmering, start the fusilli pasta. Place a large pot of water on to boil. When it reaches a boil add the kosher salt and the pasta, return to a boil, and cook according to the package directions. When the pasta is almost al dente, (tender but firm to the bite) add it to the tomatoes and the veal chops. Cover and cook the pasta in the pan with the tomatoes and chops for another 15 to 25 min. The pasta will take on the flavor of not only the tomatoes but also of the veal. This can be kept covered and warm in the oven until ready to serve. The flavor will permeate the pasta, with the rich full flavor of the veal.

## Veal Chops with Tomatoes

*Costolette con pomodori*

4 loin veal chops (about ½ inch thick)

1 Tbsp. butter

2 or 3 fresh tomatoes peeled (instructions for peeling tomatoes page 136) and coarsely chopped

1 small onion chopped

salt and freshly ground pepper to taste

Trim the fat and skin from the outside of the veal chops. Place the chops on a flat surface and pound with a mallet, or a heavy skillet a few times to ensure that the chops will be tender. Do not over pound the veal chops, you just want to just tenderize them, not flatten them. The chops should remain almost ½ inch thick. Season the chops with salt and pepper.

Heat the butter in a large skillet or sauté pan until it is hot enough to sizzle when a piece of onion is dropped into it. Add the onion and sauté until the onion is translucent. Add the veal chops and let the chops turn a light brown on one side before turning them over. The chops should turn a nice golden brown on the second side. At this point it is time to add the coarsely chopped tomatoes. Stir the tomatoes around in the butter and make sure that the chops are not sticking to the bottom of the pan. Turn the heat down to a low simmer and cover the pan. The chops should simmer for around 30 to 40 minutes. This can be kept covered and warm in the oven until you are ready to serve.

Mashed Potatoes with Leeks Sautéed in Olive Oil (page 97) make an excellent accompaniment for this dish as does Potato Croquettes (page 99), and Gratin of Celery with Béchamel (page 86) goes well also.

Scrambled Eggs (Jason's Style)

*Uova strapazzate*

This is a dish my son Jason started to make when he was quite young. Jason created a scrambled egg dish that has perfect soft curds with a beautiful texture and taste. They are the best scrambled eggs that I have ever had. Jason uses olive oil in his scrambled eggs but you may substitute butter if you wish.

4 Large eggs

2 to 3 tsp. extra virgin olive oil or butter (enough to coat the bottom of a sauté pan

Salt and freshly ground pepper to taste

2 Tbsp. finely chopped chives (optional)

Melt the butter in a medium-sized skillet. Gently add the eggs when the butter is melted and hot enough to sizzle when an egg is added to it. Beat with a fork to break the eggs up. Season with salt and pepper to taste. Once the eggs start to firm up a little, which is almost immediately start to gently stir the eggs, with a metal spatula or large spoon forming the soft curds. Add the optional chopped chives and remove from the heat as soon as the dish is holding together and has formed those luscious soft curds.

Serve with a vegetable dish such as Zucchini and Celery with Tomatoes (page 91) or Green Salad (page 164) and a slice of crusty Italian Bread (page 20) or good quality purchased Italian or French bread is very nice also.

## Scrambled Eggs with Gruyere Cheese

*Uova strapazzate con formaggio*

This recipe follows Jason's technique for scrambled eggs.

4 large eggs

2 to 3 tsp. olive oil or butter (enough to coat the bottom of a medium sized sauté pan)

2 Tbsp. finely chopped curly parsley or 2 Tbsp. finely chopped chives

¼ Lb. Gruyere cheese cut into pieces of 1 inch by 1 inch

Salt and freshly ground black pepper to taste

Place the olive oil or butter in a medium sized sauté pan and heat over medium heat. Gently add the eggs when the butter is melted and hot enough to sizzle when an egg is added to it. Beat with a fork to break the eggs up. Add the salt and pepper to taste. Once the eggs start to firm up a little, which is almost immediately start to gently stir the eggs, with a metal spatula or large spoon forming the soft curds. As soon as soft curds start forming add the cheese the parsley or chives. Continue to gently move the eggs in the pan. Remove from the heat when the eggs have reached the desired consistency and the cheese is melted. They should still be somewhat moist.

Serve with a vegetable dish such as Tomatoes and Zucchini (page 89), or a salad with a vinaigrette such as Mixed Salad (page 166).

Scrambled Eggs with Zucchini

*Uova strapazzate con* zucchine

This is a dish I enjoyed many times as a child with my Mother, Marguerite for lunch. It is a warm and homey dish that is very fast and delicious. This can be served with Italian or French bread that is sliced, buttered and then toasted in the oven. A salad of tender greens with an olive oil vinaigrette such as Green Salad (page 164) makes this meal complete and so delicious.

2 to 3 butter tsp. (enough to coat the bottom of a medium sauté pan)

4 large eggs

3 small zucchini

Salt & Freshly ground Pepper to taste

Cut the off the stem ends of the zucchini and a small slice off the bottom ends of the zucchini.

Heat the butter in a sauté pan over medium heat. Gently add the eggs when the butter is melted and starts to sizzle when an egg is added to it. Beat the eggs with a fork to break up the eggs. Add the zucchini slices immediately. Season with salt and pepper to taste. Once the eggs start to firm up a little, which is almost immediately start to gently stir the eggs, with a metal spatula or large spoon forming the soft curds. Continue to move the eggs and zucchini mixture, until the eggs have formed soft curds, and the zucchini slices are tender. Serve as soon as possible.

## Fernand's Eggs with Potatoes

*Fernand's uova strapazzate con patate*

This was one of my Uncle's favorite dishes to make for children for an easy lunch. I loved to sit down to a meal that "Uncle Fern" had prepared.

1 ½ Tbsp. butter

3 potatoes (russet)

4 large eggs beaten until the yolks and whites are blended

salt and pepper

1 Tbsp. finely chopped chives (optional)

1 Tbsp very finely chopped parsley (optional)

Peel each potato and trim into a rectangle. Slice the potato into ½ inch thick slices. Stack the slices and cut into ½ inch sticks. You should end up with sticks of about ½ by ½ by 1 ½ inches long. Heat the butter in a skillet or large sauté pan until it is hot enough to sizzle when a piece of potato is dropped into it. Add the potato sticks to the hot butter. Brown the sticks on all sides using a spatula to turn the potato sticks as necessary. When the potatoes are nicely browned on all sides and tender on the inside, add the lightly beaten eggs. The eggs should start to coagulate almost immediately. Turn the heat down to low. Use a metal spatula or spoon to stir the eggs as they are cooking. Continue to move the egg and potato mixture until the eggs have formed soft curds.

This dish can also be made into a frittata. To make this dish into a frittata do not stir the beaten eggs after you add them to the pan with the potatoes. Turn down the heat to low and let the eggs cook very slowly. The eggs will set and when the eggs have thickened and cooked and only the top is runny, take a dinner plate that is larger in circumference than you skillet and place it over your skillet and turn the skillet upside down, so that the runny side of the frittata is on the plate. Slide the frittata runny side down into the skillet and let it cook until the frittata is set all the way through.

Sole in Olive Oil and Lemon Juice

*Sogliole*

4 skinless sole fillets

extra virgin olive oil

2 lemons juiced

2 lemons cut into quarters

Pour enough olive oil into an ovenproof dish baking dish to have a depth of 1/3 inch. Rinse the fillets under cold water and place them into the olive oil in the baking dish. Season with the salt and pepper on one side, then turn over in the olive oil and season on the other side. Place into a preheated 350 degree Fahrenheit oven and bake for 5 minutes. Pour the juice from the 2 lemons over the fillets, and bake for an additional 5 minutes or so. Watch closely and when the fish is flaking remove from the oven. Serve with the quartered lemons.

A Baked Potato (page 122) is excellent with this, as is a salad with a lemon juice vinaigrette such as Tender Greens with a Lemon Juice Vinaigrette (page 165)

## Baked Fish

*Pesce al forno*

1 lb. fish fillets (halibut, haddock, or cod) cut into serving size pieces

milk for coating the fish fillets

1 ½ cup plain dried breadcrumbs page 111 for dredging

2 Tbsp. finely chopped parsley

salt and freshly ground pepper

extra virgin olive oil for coating the bottom of an oven-proof dish

1 lemon thinly sliced

2 lemons cut into wedges

Lightly coat an oven-proof dish with olive oil. Stir the chopped parsley into the breadcrumbs and place the mixture in a shallow bowl. Pour the milk into another shallow bowl. Dip each piece of fish into the bowl of milk and let the excess drip back into the bowl, then place the fish in the breadcrumbs and let the excess crumbs fall back into the breadcrumb bowl. Place the fish pieces in the olive oil coated dish. Divide the butter into small dabs of about ½ tsp. each and arrange over the fish pieces. Season with salt and pepper and place in a preheated 350 degree Fahrenheit oven. While the fish is baking thinly slice 1 of the lemons and place a lemon slice on top of each piece of fish after 25 minutes. Bake for an additional 5 to 10 minutes or until the fish flakes easily.

Remove from the oven and serve immediately, with the lemon wedges.

Cannelini Beans Drizzled with Olive Oil (page 101) makes a nice first course or just served alongside. Zucchini and Tomato Gratin (page 92) goes well as does a salad with vinaigrette such as Green Salad (page 164).

## Sardines with Zucchini

*Saraghine con zucchine*

This makes a delicious lunch or these can be used as antipasti. Toasted bread works especially well if you are using these as antipasti.

1 tin of sardines packed in olive oil

2 medium zucchinis or 3 small zucchinis

Mayonnaise page 115 or a good quality store-bought mayonnaise

several leaves of butter lettuce

2 slices good quality white or whole wheat bread, toasted if you wish, each slice cut into 4 triangles

If you are toasting the bread, place the slices of bread in a preheated 350 degree Fahrenheit oven.(Oven toasting the bread gives a more uniform toast.) Toast on one side until it is a light golden color on the bottom and then turn over and toast on the other side, about 4 to 5 minutes on each side.

Clean the sardines by removing the tails and filleting the sardines, removing the spine, and cleaning out the insides. Cut off the ends of the zucchinis, you may peel them or leave the peel on whichever is your preference. Reserve 1 small zucchini or ½ of a medium zucchini for cutting into matchstick size strips. Slice the remaining zucchinis into ¼ inch slices. Cut the slices of bread or toast into triangles by slicing each slice in half diagonally, and then in half diagonally again the other way. Tear or cut the leaves of lettuce into pieces that are about the same size as the pieces of bread. Spread the bread triangles with the mayonnaise and place a lettuce leaf on top of the mayonnaise, then place a slice or two of the zucchini on top of the lettuce, lay 2 to 4 sardine fillets on top. Scatter a few of the matchstick zucchini sticks on top of each serving.

Serves 8 as an antipasti or 4 for lunch

Salmon Patties

*Salmone polpettine*

1 cup chopped celery (about 5 stalks)

7 scallions

2 slices white or whole wheat bread (crusts removed)

1/3 to ½ cup whole milk (enough to soften the bread)

2 eggs lightly beaten

2 Tbsp. of whole wheat flour

¼ cup finely chopped parsley

salt and freshly ground pepper to taste

2 cans 6 oz. each of wild Alaskan salmon with skin and bones removed

extra virgin olive oil for sautéing

2 lemons cut into wedges (for serving with the patties)

Cut off the bottom of the celery and cut off the top ends of the celery by about ¼ of an inch, if the ends are dried out. Thoroughly rinse off the celery to remove any dirt. Remove all leaves and reserve for another use. Remove any tough strings from the stalks by placing your knife under the strings and pulling them lengthwise down the celery stalk. Or remove the strings with a vegetable peeler by shaving a thin layer off. Chop into a small dice ¼ to 1/3 inch. Cut off the bottoms of the scallions and the tough green tops. Remove the outer layer, and cut the scallions into thin slices.

Tear the bread into small pieces and place in a large bowl. Add the milk and thoroughly mush up the bread and milk with a fork. Add the lightly beaten eggs, and stir. Add the 2 tablespoons of flour, a good pinch of salt and a pinch of freshly ground pepper. Stir again and add the chopped celery, the chopped scallions, and the chopped parsley. Mix together thoroughly. Form into small patties, about 1 ½ inch in diameter.

Put enough olive oil in a large sauté pan to come up to a depth of ¼ inch. Heat the oil and when it is hot enough to sizzle when a small piece of the salmon mixture is placed in the oil, add the patties. Do not crowd. Sauté until golden brown on one side and then turn over and sauté until golden brown on other side. Remove from the oil and place on a paper towel lined plate to blot the oil off, then transfer the patties to a serving plate and serve them, or transfer to an oven proof dish and place in a warm oven until you are ready to serve them.

Serve with lemon wedges for each person. Mayonnaise (page 115) or the Aïoli on (page 116) goes very well with these patties.

Shrimp Sautéed in Butter and Garlic

*Gamberi 'Stile Scampi'*

8 colossal shrimp in the shell deveined and butterflied see instructions below

3 Tbsp butter

4 cloves garlic finely chopped

Sea salt to taste

Cut through the backside of the shell with a small sharp knife or a small sharp scissors. Start at the large end and cut down to the tail and peel the shell off, you may leave the tail on if you wish. It makes a nice presentation with the tail left on. To butterfly the shrimp, place on a flat surface and with a small knife cut partially through the back side starting at the tail end and cut lengthwise down to the large end. Do not cut through the flesh completely. If there is a dark vein remove it. Flatten out the shrimp for the butterfly shape. Heat the butter in a large skillet or sauté pan over medium high heat. Place the finely chopped garlic into the butter once it has reached the point that it sizzles when a piece of garlic is dropped into it. Sauté for a minute or so and add the shrimp. Sauté the shrimp for 2 minutes on one side and turn over and sauté on the other side until the shrimp are pink and cooked through, about another 2 or 3 minutes. Sprinkle with sea salt to taste and serve.

Artichokes with Melted Butter (page 68) go exceptionally well with this as does Gratin of Celery with Béchamel (page 86) A Baked Potato (page 122) is a nice simple accompaniment.

Roasted Crab Legs

*Granchio arrosto al forno*

The crab legs are usually pre-cooked and have only to be thoroughly heated through. This is an easy and totally delicious way of heating crab legs. The Bairdi or the Oppillio are fine. If you are using King Crab you will have to increase the heating time.

16 crab legs (for 4 legs per person)

2 Tbsp. melted butter per person

Break off the crab legs from the body of the crabs. Discard the bodies and place the legs, while still frozen on a rimmed baking sheet. They should be spread out so that the heat can circulate evenly around each crab leg. Place in a preheated 400 degree Fahrenheit oven. Turn down the heat after 7 minutes to 350 degrees and roast for another 10 minutes.

Serve each person 4 to 5 legs and give each person a small dish of melted butter to dip the crab meat into. Individual butter warmers make a nice presentation. I suggest that if you are serving children that you omit the butter warmers, as you could easily have an accident with the candles. The butter can be melted in the kitchen and poured into individual dishes or ramekins.

Serves 4

Give each person a crab cracker and pick or if you do not have these, a regular nut cracker and pick works just fine.

Artichokes with Melted butter (page 68) are a natural to go with crab legs and you can use the melted butter for both dishes.

# Salads

# Insalata

## Green Salad

*Insalata verde*

I love salads with a good deal of vinegar, and I usually use 3 parts of vinegar to 1 part olive oil. If this ratio is not to your liking reduce the amount of vinegar and increase the amount of olive oil.

1 head of butter lettuce

¼ cup red wine vinegar

1 Tbsp. extra virgin olive oil

Salt to taste (optional)

1 Tbsp. finely chopped chives (optional)

Pour the vinegar into a salad bowl, if you are using salt add it next. Stir with a fork and the salt will start to dissolve in the vinegar. Add the olive oil. Beat with a fork to combine. This is a broken dressing so that you will see the droplets of oil. It should not emulsify. Remove the outer leaves of the head of lettuce and discard. The leaves exposed at the top should be removed if they are damaged. Cut around the bottom core, remove and discard it. Place the lettuce leaves in a colander and rinse under cold water. Shake out the lettuce to remove as much water as possible. Tear into bite size pieces and place into the salad bowl and toss with the dressing.

## Tender Greens with Lemon Juice Vinaigrette

*Insalata* verde *al limone*

I use this lemon and olive oil vinaigrette on tender greens from my garden. This is a very light and refreshing salad. Any tender young butter lettuce greens are delicious with this dressing.

2 lemons

2 tablespoons extra virgin olive oil

1 head of butter lettuce or 2 cups tender young leaves of butter lettuce that have not yet formed a head

Cut the lemons in half crosswise, remove any seeds and squeeze the juice into a salad bowl. Add the olive oil. Beat with a fork to combine. This is a broken dressing so you will see droplets of oil. It should not emulsify. If you are using a head of butter lettuce, remove the outer leaves of the head of lettuce and discard. The leaves exposed at the top should be removed if they are damaged. Cut around the bottom core, remove and discard it. Place the lettuce leaves in a colander and rinse under cold water. If you are using tender young greens that have not yet formed a head, just place in a colander and rinse under cold water. Shake out the lettuce to remove as much water as possible. Tear into bite size pieces and place into the salad bowl and toss thoroughly with the dressing.

This salad goes very well with Baked Fish (page 157), or Chickpea Patties (page 104)

Mixed Salad

*Insalata mista*

This makes a great salad if you are not serving any other vegetable with your dinner. It can be made with just the extra virgin oil and vinegar of your choice or with the addition of sautéed garlic, or for a quick infusion of seasonings use the onion and garlic powder.

Vinaigrette

¾ cup balsamic vinegar or good quality red wine vinegar

¼ cup extra virgin olive oil

Optional ingredients for vinaigrette

1 tablespoon sautéed garlic (room temperature) page 106

¼ tsp. onion powder and a very small pinch of garlic powder

Salt and a pinch of white pepper or black pepper

Ingredients for salad

1 head of butter lettuce

3 medium carrots peeled rinsed and thinly sliced

5 or 6 radishes with the bottoms and tops removed, rinsed and thinly sliced

1 cup of curly endive leaves or 1 head of radicchio

1 cup young tender organic dandelion leaves (optional)

1 tbsp. chives finely chopped

For the vinaigrette

Pour the vinegar into a salad bowl large enough to accommodate all of your salad ingredients. If you are using salt and pepper, add them at this point. Stir with a fork and the salt will start to dissolve in the vinegar. Add the olive oil and beat with a fork to combine. This is a broken dressing, so that you will see the droplets of oil. It should not emulsify. If you are using the sautéed garlic or onion and garlic powder - add them at this point.

For the salad

Add the carrot and the radish slices and toss with the dressing. These are sturdy and can marinate in the dressing while you prepare the lettuce.

For the butter lettuce remove the outer leaves of the head of lettuce and discard. The leaves exposed at the top should be removed if they are damaged. Cut around the bottom core, remove and discard it.

If you are using the curly endive, cut around the bottom core remove and discard it, and tear off the leaves that you are going to use.

For the radicchio, remove the bottom core as described for the endive. Remove the outer leaves of the radicchio and discard. If you are using the dandelion leaves just remove any damaged leaves.

Rinse all the lettuce leaves in a colander under cold water. Shake out the lettuce to remove as much water as possible. Tear into bite size pieces and place into the salad bowl and toss with the dressing.

Add the optional chives, and gently toss everything together.

## Celery and Chicken in a Vinaigrette

*Insalata di sedano con pollo*

After my Grandmother came to this country, she started a tradition of serving this salad the day after Thanksgiving, using leftover turkey from her recipe: Turkey Stuffed with Black Olives page 145. This salad is a wonderful way to use leftovers from a roasted turkey or a roasted chicken such as Roast Chicken page 144.

Vinaigrette

¾ cup apple cider vinegar

¼ cup extra virgin olive oil

freshly ground pepper to taste

Ingredients for salad

1 ½ cups chopped celery (1 bunch celery)

¾ cup cold cooked chicken or turkey (meat from the breast works best for this salad)

4 scallions (optional)

For the vinaigrette

Pour the apple cider vinegar into a salad bowl large enough to accommodate all of your salad ingredients. Add the olive oil, and beat with a fork to combine. This is a broken dressing, so that you will see the droplets of oil. It should not emulsify.

For the salad

Remove the root end of the celery and cut off the tips by about ¼ of an inch, if the tips are dried out. Thoroughly rinse off the celery to remove any dirt. Remove all tough strings from the stalks by placing your knife under the strings and pulling them lengthwise down the celery stalk. Or remove the strings with a vegetable peeler by shaving a thin layer off. Cut into a medium dice of 1/3 to ½ inch including the leaves. If you are using the optional scallions cut off the bottoms of the scallions and the tough green tops. Remove the outer layer, and then cut the scallions into thin slices.

Add the celery and the scallions to the vinaigrette. These are sturdy and can marinate while you prepare the chicken or turkey. Chop the chicken or turkey into pieces of about 1 inch. Add the pieces and toss to coat with the vinaigrette.

Potatoes Roasted with Olive Oil (page 93), or Oven Crisped Potatoes (page 94) goes well with this salad. This salad also makes a great light lunch served with Toasted Garlic Bread (page 7).

Salad Croutons

*Pane al forno*

These also can be used as a topping on soups. They go especially well with Squash Soup on page 36.

½ loaf of Italian Bread page 20 or good quality purchased Italian or French bread

6 Tbsp. butter

Sea salt and freshly ground pepper to taste

Melt the butter over medium heat making sure not to burn the butter, set it aside to cool until it is just warm. Slice the bread into ½ inch slices and then the cut the slices into 1nch pieces. Place the bread into a bowl and pour the warm butter over the bread. Add the sea salt and pepper and mix to coat the bread on all sides. Spread the bread on a baking sheet and place in a preheated 350 degree Fahrenheit oven. Bake for 4 to 5 minutes and then turn the bread pieces over, bake another 4 to 5 minutes and turn the bread over again. Check after another minute or so, the bread should be golden and totally dried out. Total baking time will be about 15 minutes. Remove from the oven and let them cool.

# Cheese Course

## *Formaggio*

Cheese with Fruit and Nuts

*Formaggio al frutta mista e noci*

This makes a beautiful close to a meal. Italians love great desserts, but they are not served everyday. Most Italian meals end with cheese and fruit. Placing the cheese on cake stands makes an elegant presentation. You can use just 2 or 3 cheeses and 1 or 2 types of nuts and 1 or 2 types of fruit if you wish. If you are serving a celebratory meal for many people, it is a good idea to have many choices. During the cold months fresh organic berries and melons are not always available and I prefer and you may also prefer to use pears, apples and dried figs. Also, the pears apples and dried figs are a welcome addition at any time of year.

½ lb Parmigiano-Reggiano

1/3 lb. Gorgonzola

1/3 lb. Camembert

1/3 lb. Gruyere

1/3 lb Provolone

1 cup toasted walnuts page 120

½ cup whole almonds with their skins on

½ cup whole hazelnuts

1 cup fresh organic blueberries

1 cup fresh organic strawberries

1 cup fresh organic raspberries

1 cup fresh cantaloupe or Tuscan cantaloupe cut into balls with a melon scoop

2 fresh pears peeled and sliced

2 apples peeled or unpeeled and sliced

1 cup dried figs

Pry off small bite-size chunks of Parmigiano with a cheese knife or small sturdy sharp knife. Cut the Gorgonzola into small bite-size chunks and cut the remainder of the cheeses into small bite-size squares. Arrange attractively on a raised cake plate or other plate. Place the nuts into small bowls and serve with spoons for your family and friends to serve themselves. Rinse the fruits under cold running water. Hull the strawberries if you wish. Then place the fruits in bowls or on plates, be sure to serve with a small tongs and spoons or toothpicks to make it easy for everyone to serve themselves.

This course can be served with a sparkling water such as Pellegrino, or a sparkling wine such as an Italian Prosecco, or a wine, such as a dry sherry or a dry Marsala.

Parmesan with Strawberries and Balsamic Vinegar

*Fragolini Parmigiani*

½ lb wedge Parmigiano-Reggiano

1 cup fresh strawberries

fine quality balsamic vinegar (aceto balsamico) it should be from Modena Italy and be aged in wood barrels at least 12 years

Pry off small bite-size chunks of Parmigiano with a cheese knife or a small sturdy knife. Arrange on a serving plate. Rinse the strawberries under cold running water, and you may hull the strawberries if you wish. Add the strawberries to the serving plate with the Parmigiano and arrange attractively.

Sprinkle the balsamic vinegar over the cheese chunks and strawberries.

# Sweets

## *Dolce*

Celebration White Cake with Cherry and Walnut Filling and Cherry Frosting

*Torta*

This cake makes a wonderful birthday cake. It has been used for birthdays in my family for several generations. It is made up of 3 layers so it makes a tall and beautiful presentation. This cake is perfect without any flavoring, but you may use the optional almond extract, if you wish.

1 1/8 cup butter softened

2 ¼ cups sugar

¼ tsp. almond extract (optional)

3 3/8 cups all purpose flour* page 178

4½ tsp. baking powder

1 ½ cups whole milk

8 egg whites

Grease and lightly dust with flour 3 9x1 ½ inch round cake pans. Mix together the flour and baking powder and sift. In a separate large bowl cream the butter and sugar together until the mixture is light colored and fluffy. This can be done in an electric mixer or with a hand held mixer. Add the almond extract at this point if you are using it. Now, add about ¼ of the sifted dry ingredients to the creamed mixture and add alternately with milk. Beat well after each addition, making sure to end by adding dry ingredients. Beat the egg whites in a clean dry bowl with a clean dry beater until they form stiff peaks, and then add the egg whites to the batter by gently folding them in. Bake in a preheated 375 degree Fahrenheit oven for 18 to 20 minutes or until a toothpick comes out clean when inserted into the middle of the pan. Cool for approximately 10 minutes and invert onto cooling racks. Cool thoroughly before frosting.

Maraschino Cherry Frosting

4 egg whites

2 ½ cups granulated sugar

½ cup powdered sugar

4 tsp. light corn syrup

2/3 cup cold water

½ tsp. almond extract

1 Tbsp. maraschino cherry juice, or enough to give the frosting and filling a light pink color.

Alternatively you cam omit the almond extract, and increase the Maraschino cherry juice to 3 Tbsp.

Place the egg whites, granulated sugar, corn syrup, and water in the top of a double boiler, or a bowl that will fit on top of a pan of boiling water. Before placing on top of the boiling water beat ½ minute on low speed of an electric mixer or beat with a balloon whisk to blend ingredients together. Now, place the top of the double boiler or the bowl over boiling water, but not touching the water. Beat constantly with a hand held mixer or a balloon whisk till the frosting forms stiff peaks. This will take between 10 and 15 minutes. Remove from the boiling water and add the optional almond extract if you are using it, and the maraschino cherry juice. Mix until thoroughly blended. Reserve 2/3 of the mixture for the frosting and use the remaining third for the following filling recipe.

Maraschino Cherry and Walnut Filling

1/3 of the above frosting

5 jars 6 oz. each (30 oz.) maraschino cherries roughly chopped (each cherry should be chopped into fourths.)

12 oz. walnuts (roughly chopped)

Add the chopped cherries and chopped walnuts to the frosting and mix.

Assembly

Place the bottom cake layer on a serving plate. Spread ½ of the filling over the cake layer. Place the second cake layer on top of the filling. Spread the remaining filling on top of this layer. Place the third cake layer on top of the filling. Spread the top and sides of the cake with the reserved frosting, using a 1 inch wide offset spatula or a table knife. Make some free form swirls on the top of the cake. Bellissimo!

*Be sure to use all-purpose flour. The all-purpose flour makes a perfect crumb for this cake.

Serve this with vanilla ice-cream. Pastry Cream (page 183) also goes beautifully with this cake.

A tall domed cake stand is an excellent way to store this cake. If you do not have one, just cover the cake with plastic wrap. Store in the refrigerator. This cake keeps very well for several days.

Cream Puffs

*Pasticcini ripieni*

Cream Puff Pastry – Pasta Soffiata

Sweetened Whipped Cream – Pana Montata page 181 or Coffee Flavored Whipped Cream page 182

Pastry Cream – Crema pasticcera page 183

You may fill the puffs with the Sweetened Whipped Cream,or the Coffee Whipped Cream or the delicate Pastry Cream or a combination of either of the whipped creams with the Pastry Cream. The puff pastry is basically the same dough as for the Gruyere Puffs, without the pepper or the cheese and with the addition of sugar.

For the Puff Pastry (Pate au Choux) – Pasta Soffiata

9 Tbsp. butter

1 ½ cups water

2 tsp. sugar

pinch of salt

1 1/2 cups unbleached all-purpose flour

5 large eggs

butter for coating 2 baking sheets

For the Egg Glaze

1 egg

1 tsp. cold water

Lightly butter 2 baking sheets and set aside. Measure out the flour and set aside. Place the butter, water, sugar, and salt in a saucepan and bring to a boil over high heat. When the butter is melted and the water is bubbling, immediately remove the saucepan from the heat. Stir in the flour all at once. Beat the mixture vigorously with a wooden spoon to blend thoroughly. Place over moderate heat and continue to beat vigorously until the mixture leaves the side of the pan and forms a ball, and starts to form a film on the bottom of the pan. Remove from the heat, and make an indention in the dough, and place an egg into it. Stir vigorously to incorporate, then, add the remaining eggs 1 at a time stirring vigorously after each egg. Use 2 tablespoons to drop mounds of Pasta Soffiata that are 1 to ½ inches in diameter and 1 inch high onto your 2 lightly buttered baking sheets. The mounds should be at least 1 ½ inches apart.

Beat the egg and 1 tsp. cold water for the egg glaze, and brush over the tops of the dough mounds. Do not let the glaze dribble down the sides of the mounds onto the baking sheets as this will prevent them from rising. Place in a preheated 400 degree Fahrenheit oven. Bake for about 20 minutes. They may take a minute or two longer. They should turn a golden brown and be crisp to the touch. Turn the heat down to 350 degrees and bake 10 minutes more. Let them cool down until they are just warm, and fill with Sweetened Whipped Cream (page 181), or Coffee Flavored Whipped Cream (page 182), or Pastry Cream (page 183) or a combination of any of these. To add a filling to the puffs cut a horizontal slit in the side of each puff. If the puffs have to much soft dough in them, just take out the excess dough with a small spoon or your fingers. With a small spoon fill each puff with about a teaspoonful of filling.

Makes 35 to 40 small puffs.

Sweetened Whipped Cream

*Panna montata*

1 pint (2 cups) heavy whipping cream

¼ cup plus 2 Tbsp. powdered sugar

1 Tbsp. to 1 Tbsp. plus 2 tsp. vanilla extract (to taste)

The cream should be well chilled just from the refrigerator (under 40 degrees F.) Beat with an electric hand mixer if you have one, otherwise a stand mixer or a whisk. Start beating slowly so that the cream does not spray out of the bowl. Beat until the cream is thickened, then add the powdered sugar and mix until combined. Add the Tbsp. of vanilla extract and stir until it is mixed in thoroughly. Taste and add more if needed. The cream should form soft peaks when the beater is slowly lifted up. Place in the refrigerator and let it sit for at least an hour before serving to let the flavors meld.

Tip: Beating the cream before adding the flavorings lets maximum air to be incorporated into the cream.

## Coffee Flavored Whipped Cream

*Panna di caffe*

### Method I

1 recipe Sweetened Whipped Cream page 181

2 Tbsp. very strong coffee or espresso that has been cooled

Follow the recipe for Sweetened Whipped Cream, but use only 2 tsp. of vanilla extract, and fold in thoroughly 2 tbsp. very strong coffee or espresso.

### Method II

1 recipe Sweetened Whipped Cream page 181

2 tsp instant coffee crystals

Before making the Sweetened Whipped Cream, reserve 4 tsp. of the heavy whipping cream and dissolve the instant coffee crystals in the reserved cream, and set aside. Prepare the Sweetened Whipped Cream. Fold in the cream coffee crystal mixture and mix thoroughly.

## Pastry Cream

*Crema pasticcera*

6 egg yolks

½ cup sugar

½ cup unbleached all-purpose flour

2 cups milk

2 Tbsp. butter

1Tbsp. to 1 Tbsp. plus 1 tsp. pure vanilla extract (to taste)

Heat the milk in a heavy bottomed saucepan, and in another heavy bottomed saucepan (off the heat) beat the egg yolks with a wire whisk, while gradually adding the sugar. Beat until the yolks are a pale yellow color and when the whisk is lifted it forms a slowly dissolving ribbon as it falls back into the mixture. Whisk in the flour and then pour the hot milk in very slowly, in a thin stream. Place over moderate heat and beat vigorously to smooth out all the lumps. Turn the heat down to low, and stir continuously for about 2 minutes, or until the mixture starts to thicken (being very careful not to let the mixture start to burn on the bottom). The mixture will thicken more as it cools, so it is very important not to overcook the pastry cream.

Remove from the heat and add the butter, while beating vigorously, and add 1 Tbsp of vanilla extract. Taste to see if it needs an additional ½ to 1 tsp. vanilla.

Strawberries and Cream

*Fragole di panna*

1 pint strawberries

2 to 3 Tbsp. sugar

1 recipe Sweetened Whipped Cream page 181

Rinse the strawberries and cut the tops off. Place the strawberries in a glass bowl and sprinkle the sugar over them. Place in the refrigerator, and let them macerate for at least 2 hours.

Prepare the Sweetened Whipped Cream and place in the refrigerator for at least an hour to let the flavors meld.

Serve the strawberries in a dessert cup or a stemmed glass such as a martini glass. Spoon the juices that have formed over the strawberries. Top each serving with a dollop of Sweetened Whipped Cream.

Blueberry Dessert Sauce

*Salsa di mirtilli*

1 pint fresh blueberries or frozen blueberries

1/3 cup sugar

If you are using fresh blueberries rinse them in a colander and remove any stems. Place the fresh or frozen blueberries in a 1 quart saucepan and add the sugar on top of them. Place over med-high heat and stir frequently to make sure the blueberries do not stick to the bottom of the pan or start to burn. Let the sauce come to a boil and then reduce the heat to a very low simmer. Let simmer stirring occasionally for ten minutes. Turn the heat off and let it cool.

This may be served warm or at room temperature or cold. If you are not using the sauce once it has cooled somewhat, you can place this sauce in the refrigerator until you are ready to use it. It is delicious cold. This will keep for 3 to 4 days in the refrigerator. It is delicious in Blueberry Ice-Cream Dessert (page 186) or served as a topping for ice cream, or served with a dollop of Sweetened Whipped Cream (page 181).

Blueberry Ice Cream Dessert

*Mirtilli dolce*

This is a simple delicious dessert that has been served by several generations in my family. Once the Blueberry Sauce and ice cream is mixed together, it should have a thick texture, be purple in color with the blueberries strewn throughout the whole dessert.

1 recipe Blueberry Dessert Sauce page 185

1 pint ice cream

Place a scoop or two of vanilla ice cream in a dessert cup or a stemmed glass such as a martini glass. Place a Tbsp or so of the Blueberry Sauce on the ice cream and thoroughly mix them together until the mixture is thick and thoroughly combined. If it seems thin add a little more ice cream and mix thoroughly.

This seems to work better when mixed in individual servings. Do not blend in a blender, as it tears up the blueberries and gives a different texture and taste.

## Raspberry Whipped Cream

*Lampone di panna*

This makes a really beautiful dessert. You can use stemmed wide mouthed glasses such as martini glasses, or burgundy wineglasses, or small footed dessert dishes to serve this in. It makes a great presentation.

1 recipe Sweetened Whipped Cream page 181

1 cup fresh raspberries (rinsed)

plus raspberries for garnish

Prepare the Sweetened Whipped Cream. Place it in the refrigerator.

Puree the raspberries in a food processor. Press through a fine strainer to remove the seeds. You may add a little sugar (1 to 2 tsp.) to taste if you wish. Divide the puree in half.

Divide the Sweetened Whipped Cream in half and set ½ aside. Take the second half, and divide that in half. Take 1 part of the divided half and mix with ½ of the raspberry puree, to make a raspberry cream. Take the other part of the divided half of the Sweetened Whipped Cream and gently fold in the second half of the raspberry puree to form swirls.

### To Serve

Place a dollop of the swirled raspberry cream on the bottom of each dessert dish. Top that with a dollop of the raspberry cream. Take the reserved Sweetened Whipped Cream and spoon a dollop of it on top of each dessert dish. Place a few raspberries on each dish and serve.

Marguerite's Sugar Cookies

*Biscotti allo zucchero*

These are a great holiday cookie, as well as a very refreshing sweet on a warm summer's day. I have made these since childhood and they are still a favorite of mine.

1 ½ cup sugar

1 cup butter

2 eggs

3 cups flour

1 tsp. baking powder

1 tsp. baking soda

pinch of salt

1 ½ tsp. pure vanilla extract

sugar for the tops of the cookies

walnuts for the tops of the cookies

maraschino cherries for the tops of the cookies

reserved juice from the maraschino cherries (optional)

Lightly butter a cookie sheet and set aside. Cream the butter and sugar together in a large bowl. Lightly beat the eggs in a small bowl and add them to the butter sugar mixture. In a separate bowl mix together the flour, baking powder, baking soda, and salt. Add the flour mixture to the butter, sugar, and egg mixture. Blend thoroughly and add the vanilla extract. Roll into 1 inch balls and place on your lightly buttered cookie sheet. Dip the bottom of a glass which has a diameter of around 2 inches into a plate of sugar, and then flatten each ball of cookie dough into a cookie the size of your glass. Repeat dipping into the sugar before flattening each cookie. Sprinkle a little additional sugar on each cookie. Place ½ of a maraschino cherry or a walnut half on top of each cookie. You may drizzle a little of the reserved juice from the maraschino cherries on some of the cookies if you wish. Place in a preheated 350 degree Fahrenheit oven for about 15 minutes. Remove from the oven when they are still quite light in color. The bottoms of the cookies should be a very light golden brown, and the tops should remain white.

## Lemon Meringues

*Meringa al lemone*

These are so light and airy. Their tenderness comes from the addition of powered sugar. These are wonderful with ice cream and berries, or Pastry Cream page 183, and berries, or any ice especially the Lemon Ice page 192.

4 egg whites - ½ liquid cup

½ cup granulated sugar

1 cup powdered sugar

1 ½ tsp. lemon zest (preferably organic)

2 ½ tsp. freshly squeezed lemon juice

butter for coating a large cookie sheet

Prepare a large cookie sheet by coating it with butter and set aside. Place the egg whites in the bowl of a mixer and let them sit out for 10 to 15 minutes to bring them up to room temperature. Beat on medium speed until the egg whites are foamy, add a few drops of the lemon juice and increase the speed to high speed. When the egg whites begin to form soft peaks, you can gradually add the granulated sugar a tablespoon at a time while beating on high speed. When the whites hold stiff peaks and are glossy, stop beating, and sprinkle the powered sugar over the egg whites ¼ cup at a time, and with a large silicon or rubber spatula, fold the powdered sugar into the egg whites. When the sugar has been folded in, you may fold in the rest of the lemon juice and lemon the zest.

Place by teaspoonfuls on the prepared baking sheets. Place in a preheated 200 degree Fahrenheit oven. Bake for 2 ½ to 3 hours. then turn the oven off and leave the meringues in the oven to dry out for another 3 hours.

These should remain white, if they start to turn a light beige turn the heat off and let them continue to dry out in the oven with the heat off.

This recipe can be doubled, but you will have to move the cookie sheets around in the oven to ensure even baking. Switch the sheets from top to bottom and vice versa after 1 hour of baking.

Lemon Ice – Lemon Sorbet

*Granita al Limone*

Granitas can be served as a palate cleanser between courses, or as refreshing snack, or a light after dinner desert. This is a favorite of mine which I make all year long.

¼ cup sugar

1 cup water

½ cup freshly squeezed lemon juice

Place the sugar and the water in a saucepan over medium heat. Stir often until the sugar is dissolved. Bring the mixture to a boil and let it boil for about 1 minute until the syrup is sparklingly clear. Let the syrup cool to room temperature. Pour the lemon juice through a fine sieve to catch any small seeds and pulp. Once the lemon juice has been sieved, add it to the syrup and mix together. Pour into a shallow glass or other non-reactive baking dish and place in the freezer. Scrape up the ice mixture with a fork after 20 minutes. It should be starting to freeze and be somewhat slushy at this point. Leave in the freezer another 20 to 30 min. and scrape up the mixture again with the tines of a fork. Repeat twice more or until it has the texture of shaved ice, and serve.

This ice can also be served while it is still somewhat slushy. A great way to serve this is in a 2 piece ice serving set with ice in the lower bowl, and the granita in the top piece.

## Candied Flowers

*Bonbon di pratoline*

These make a lovely garnish for Lemon Ice on page 192, or vanilla ice cream. They can be placed on top of a cake for a stunning appearance.

5 to 10 flowers such as organic pansies or organic violas, or other organic edible flowers. Rose petals are also very nice, just make sure that they are organic (that they have not been treated with pesticides).

Leave the stems on the flowers and rinse the flowers under cold water. Place on paper toweling or a clean tea towel to dry. If you are using rose petals you can use a small tongs to hold on to the petal while the petals are being dipped for either method below.

### Egg White Method

1 lightly beaten pasteurized egg white

½ cup sugar for dipping the flowers (preferably super fine)

Dip the flowers, holding on to the stems, one at a time into the egg white and then into the sugar, making sure the egg white and the sugar cover both sides of the flowers. If you are having trouble getting the sugar to adhere to the flowers, you may paint the egg white on to the flowers with a small pastry brush.

Simple Syrup Method

½ cup sugar

¼ cup water

½ cup sugar for dipping the flowers (preferably superfine)

Mix sugar and water in a small saucepan, and place over medium heat. Stir often until sugar is dissolved. Bring the mixture to a boil and let it boil for about 1 minute until the syrup is sparklingly clear.

Let the syrup cool to room temperature. Dip the flowers one at a time into the syrup and then into the sugar, making sure the syrup and the sugar cover both sides of the flowers. If you are having trouble getting the syrup to adhere to the flowers, you may paint the syrup on to the flowers with a small pastry brush, just as mentioned in the above egg white method. Place on a baking sheet and let dry in the refrigerator. These last for a couple of days.

## Blueberry Pie

*Torta di mirtilli*

This pie is wonderful when fresh blueberries are available, but do not hesitate to prepare this pie with canned blueberries. They make a delicious pie filling.

4 cups fresh blueberries (preferably organic), or 1 15 ounce can (preferably organic) blueberries drained.

1 recipe for Pastry For a Two Crust Pie page 199

¾ cup sugar

2 Tbsp. all purpose flour

1 Tbsp butter

whole milk or cream for brushing on top of pie.

sugar for sprinkling on top of pie crust.

Prepare Pastry for a Two Crust Pie.

Mix the sugar and flour together. If you are using fresh blueberries rinse them and pick over the berries to remove any stem pieces. Place the berries into the sugar and flour mixture and mix together until all the berries are coated well with the sugar and flour mixture. Pour the coated blueberries into a pastry lined pie plate or tart pan. Cut the butter into several pieces and dot the blueberries with it. Cover the filling with the top pastry and seal the edges of the pie. Use a pastry brush to coat the top of the pie with whole milk or cream. Sprinkle some sugar over the top of the pie, and with a knife, make a few slits in the top crust to let steam escape. Place the pie in a preheated 400 degree Fahrenheit oven, and bake for 45 to 50 minutes. Check on the pie after the first 15 minutes of baking to make sure it is not browning too fast, and if it is, the heat can be turned down to 350 degrees Fahrenheit for the remainder of the baking time.

The pie should turn a beautiful golden color on both the top and bottom crusts. Carefully remove the pie from the oven and let it cool until the pie is just warm.

Serve with Sweetened Whipped Cream, (page 181), and or vanilla ice cream.

Tip: A glass pie plate is best to use, so that you can see color of the bottom crust and judge when the pie is done.

## Fresh Peach Pie

*Torta di pesca fresca*

Excellent fresh peaches are available in late August and early Sept., from Colorado and Washington state.

Pastry For a Two Crust Pie page 199

4 cups peeled and cut up fresh peaches

1 to 2 Tbsp. lemon juice (only if the peaches are too bland and they need the lemon juice to brighten their flavor).

3 Tbsp. unbleached all-purpose flour

1 cup sugar

2 Tbsp. butter

whole milk or cream for brushing on top of pie

sugar for sprinkling on top of pie

Prepare pastry for a double crust pie.

Mix together the 3 Tbsp. flour and the 1 cup of sugar, and set aside. Peel the peaches (a disposable plastic knife such as one you would take on a picnic does a great job of removing the peach skins, without having to blanch the peaches). A small paring knife will do the job also. Cut the peaches into fairly small chunks. If the peaches are too bland and dry, add the optional lemon juice. Add the flour sugar mixture to the peaches and mix together until all the peaches are well coated with the flour sugar mixture. Place the bottom crust in a pie plate and fill with the peach mixture. Cut up the 2 Tbsp. of butter into small pieces and dot the peaches with it. Cover the filling with the top pastry and seal the edges of the pie. Use a pastry brush to coat the top of the pie with whole milk or cream. Sprinkle some sugar over the top of the pie, and with a knife make a few slits in the top crust to allow steam to escape. Place in a preheated 400 degree Fahrenheit oven and bake for 15 minutes, then turn down the heat to 350 degrees and bake for an additional 40 to 50 minutes, until the crust is a golden color on both the top and bottom of the pie. Carefully remove the pie from the oven and let it cool until the pie is just warm.

Serve with Sweetened Whipped Cream, (page 181), and or vanilla ice cream.

Tip: A glass pie plate is best to use, so that you can see color of the bottom crust and judge when the pie is done.

Pastry For A Two Crust Pie

*Pasta per torta*

This pie pastry is delicious with its all butter fat content, and very tender because 1/3 of the flour is cake flour.

Tip: A glass pie plate is best to use, so that you can see color of the bottom crust and judge when the pie is done.

2 cups unbleached all-purpose flour

1 cup cake flour

½ tsp. salt

1 cup butter

8 to 10 Tbsp. ice water

Mix flour and salt together in a large bowl. Cut in the butter with 2 knives until the pieces are small enough to be cut in with a pastry blender. Blend until half the butter is the size of small peas and the rest resembles coarse meal. Add about 1/3 of the water and mix with a fork. Continue adding a little water at a time and mix with your hands until the dough holds together and can be formed into a ball. Do not over mix as this will give you tough dough. For the final blending, place the dough on a lightly floured surface. Take ½ of the dough and with the heal of your hand rapidly press the dough down and away from you in a firm quick smear of about 6 inches, set aside and smear the other half of the dough. Form the dough into 2 flat round discs and wrap with plastic wrap and place in the refrigerator to rest for at least 1 hour, 2 hours is preferable. The dough can be left in the refrigerator overnight.

Flour your work surface and your rolling pin lightly and flour the disc of pastry lightly also. Flatten a disc by hitting a rolling pin onto the surface 3 times in one direction and then 3 times in the opposite direction. Roll the dough out from the center until the dough is about 1/8 inch thick and large enough to fit into a pie plate or tart pan with overlap. Fold the dough in half and fit into a pie plate or tart pan. Repeat the rolling procedure with the second disc and fold it in half and lift over the pie that you have filled with your desired filling and follow directions for baking as recommended.

Warm Figs with Honey, Raisins and Lemon

*Fichi con budino*

This is a great dessert to serve in the fall. It is so warm and comforting. A light sugar cookie goes well with this, as does a glass of dry Marsala wine.

5 fresh figs cut into bite size pieces

½ cup honey

¼ cup freshly squeezed lemon juice

zest from ¼ of an organic lemon

½ cup light or dark raisins or a combination of both

Place all of the ingredients in a non-reactive saucepan and cook over moderate heat until the figs are quite soft and broken up. Remove from the heat and cool until the mixture is just warm and serve. This looks very pretty served in a martini glass or a footed dessert dish.

Index

## Appitizers - *Antipasti*

Antipasti of Crudites and Olive Oil, 2

Beans Wrapped in Prosciutto, 6

Cheese Crisps, 9

Endive with Avocado and Sour Cream, 4

Layered Potato Chips with Herbs, 11

Olives Baked in Pastry, 18

Potato Chips, 10

Prosciutto Wrapped Fruit Slices, 5

Swiss or Gruyere Cheese Puffs, 13

Swiss or Gruyere Cheese Puffs with Asparagus, 15

Toasted Garlic Bread, 7

Toasted Garlic Bread with Fresh Tomatoes and Ricotta Salata, 8

Tuscan Oranges, 3

## Bread and Pizza – Pane - Pizza

Italian Bread, 20

Margherita Pizza, 24

Olive Oil Pizza, 22

Tomato Cheese Pizza, 26

## Soups- *Zuppa*

Brown Chicken Stock, 30

Leek and Potato Soup, 34

Leek Broth, 32

Squash Soup, 36

## First Courses – *Primi Piatti*

Eggplant Lasagne, 53

Fettuccine Tossed in Cream and Butter with Parmigiano, 57

Fettuccini with Capers, Black Olives, Mushrooms and Parsley, 38

Fresh Tomato Sauce, 42

Fusilli with Roasted Tomatoes, 54

Lasagne with Marinara Sauce, 52

Linguine and Peppers, 55

Linguini with Lemon Juice, Parsley and Black Olives, 40

Linguine with Prosciutto, Peas and Parmigiano, 59

Marinara Sauce, 44

Meatballs, 50

Pasta in a Garlic Olive Oil and Butter Breadcrumb Sauce, 61

Red Clam Sauce with Linguini, 62

Risotto with Mushrooms and Peas, 65

Spaghetti with Garlic Olive Oil, and Pepperoncino, 41

Spaghetti with Tomato Meat Sauce, 47

## Side Dishes – Vegetable Dishes- *Contorni*

Artichokes with Melted Butter, 68

Asparagus with Olive Oil, 73

Broccoli with Olive Oil, 70

Brussels Sprouts in Parchment Packages, 79

Brussels Sprouts Roasted in Olive Oil, 78

Buttered Leeks, 87

Cannellini Beans Drizzled with Olive Oil, 101

Cannellini Beans with Sage Olive Oil, 103

Carrots Roasted with Olive Oil, 77

Celery Fried in Olive Oil, 83

Celery with Tomatoes, 90

Chickpea Patties - Garbanzo Patties, 104

Eggplant Lasagne, 76

Fried Zucchini Flowers and Zucchini Slices, 81

Golden Eggplant Slices, 75

Gratin of Celery with Béchamel, 86

Green Beans with Butter, 71

Green Tomatoes Fried in Olive Oil, 74

Mashed Potatoes with Sautéed Leeks, 97

Oven Crisped Potatoes, 94

Potato Croquettes, 99

Potato Gratin, 95

Potatoes Crisped with Butter, 96

Potatoes Roasted with Olive Oil, 93

Roasted Chickpeas, 106

Roasted Garlic, 88

Sautéed Spinach, 72

Simple Brussels Sprouts, 80

Simple Celery, 85

Tomatoes and Zucchini, 89

Zucchini and Celery with Tomatoes, 91

Zucchini and Tomato Gratin, 92

## Miscellaneous – *Aggegi vari*

Aïoli, 116

Baked Potatoes, 122

Béchamel, 119

Breadcrumbs, 111

How to Supreme an Orange or Grapefruit, 108

Light Dip, 118

Mayonnaise, 115

Sautéed Garlic, 109

Sautéed Leeks, 110

Sour Cream and Onion Dip, 117

Toasted Pine Nuts, 121

Toasted Walnuts, 120

## Entrees – *Secondi Piatti*

Apricot Glazed Chicken Breasts or Orange Glazed Chicken Breasts, 140

Baked Fish, 157

Beef Tenderloin with Crispy Potato Cakes, 126

Beef Tenderloin with Mushrooms, 127

Calves Liver with Butter, 147

Chicken Breasts in Sherry, 142

Chicken with Plum Tomatoes and Fusilli, 135

Chicken with Tomato Sauce and Fusilli, 138

Fernand's Eggs with Potatoes, 154

Lamb Chops Sautéed with Garlic, 131

Lamb Stew, 129

Leg of Lamb with Roasted Potatoes, 133

Roast Chicken, 144

Roasted Crab Legs, 162

Salmon Patties, 159

Sardines with Zucchini, 158

Scrambled Eggs (Jason's Style), 151

Scrambled Eggs with Gruyere Cheese, 152

Scrambled Eggs with Zucchini, 153

Shrimp Sautéed in Butter and Garlic, 161

Sole in Olive Oil and Lemon Juice, 156

Standing Rib Roast with Roasted Potatoes, 124

Turkey Stuffed with Black Olives, 145

Veal Chops with Tomatoes, 150

Veal Chops with Tomatoes and Fusilli Pasta, 148

## Salads – *Insalata*

Celery and Chicken in a Vinaigrette, 168

Croutons, 170

Green Salad, 164

Mixed Salad, 166

Tender Greens with Lemon Juice Vinaigrette, 165

## Cheese Course - *Formaggio*

Cheese with Fruit and Nuts, 172

Parmesan with Strawberries and Balsamic Vinegar, 174

## Sweets - *Dolci*

Blueberry Dessert Sauce, 185

Blueberry Ice Cream Dessert, 186

Blueberry Pie, 195

Candied Flowers, 193

Celebration White Cake with Cherry and Walnut Filling and Cherry Frosting, 176

Coffee Flavored Whipped Cream, 182

Cream Puffs, 179

Fresh Peach Pie, 197

Lemon Ice, 192

Lemon Meringues, 190

Marguerite's Sugar Cookies, page 188

Pastry Cream, 183

Pastry for a Two Crust Pie, 199

Raspberry Whipped Cream, 187

Strawberries and Cream, 184

Sweetened Whipped Cream, 181

Warm Figs with Honey, Raisins and Lemons, 201

15665907R00115

Made in the USA
Charleston, SC
14 November 2012